This book is dedicated to diggers of all ages, everywhere.
The best fossils are still in the ground.

Published by the Denver Museum of Nature & Science and People's Press

DENVER MUSEUM OF
NATURE & SCIENCE

2001 Colorado Boulevard, Denver, Colorado 80205, www.DMNS.org

People's Press
Minds Wide Open

Post Office Box 5, Aspen, Colorado 81612, www.PeoplesPress.org

Distributed by Globe Pequot Press, www.globepequotpress.com

People's Press Editorial Board Christine Benedetti, Catherine Lutz, Mirte Mallory, Nicole Beinstein Strait, George Stranahan, Craig Wheeless

Photographs by Kirk Johnson, Rick Wicker, © Denver Museum of Nature & Science, except as noted in Acknowledgments

Illustrations by Greg Michaels, Marjorie C. Leggitt, Ray Troll, and Jan Vriesen

Book design by Craig Wheeless, Rainy Day Designs

Editing by Catherine Lutz, People's Press

Proofreading by Faith Marcovecchio

Indexing by Douglas Easton

Book production by Mirte Mallory, People's Press

Book project management for Denver Museum of Nature & Science by Betsy R. Armstrong

Typeset in Adobe Cronos

Printed by Friesens in Canada

Library of Congress Control Number: 2012932688

ISBN-13: 978-1-936905-06-5

Cover: Mammoth, Snowmass ski area, and Dane Miller shouldering a mastodon femur. *Inside front cover* (left to right): Lesley Petrie, Adam Freierman, Kit Hamby, Liz Miller, Joe Enzer, and Heather Finlayson. *Page 142 and inside back cover* (left to right): Joe Sertich, Jeff Stephenson, Jack Thompson, and Mark Hunter. *Back cover:* Hannah O'Neill grapples a mastodon femur.

Opposite: Intern #3 Kaitlin Stanley holds a mastodon femur.

To Holly – Thanks for all your hard work! Kirk

To Holly – Thank you so much for the great job! Ian

Digging
Snowmastodon
Discovering an Ice Age World in the Colorado Rockies

Kirk Johnson and Ian Miller
DENVER MUSEUM OF NATURE & SCIENCE

INTRODUCTION

I am a paleontologist, and there is nothing I enjoy more than finding fossils. Two thousand and ten had been a frustrating year, filled more with paperwork and personnel hassles than with fieldwork, and to top it off, I was about to turn 50. It was September 16, and I had flown to Rapid City to participate in the Mountain-Plains Museum Association annual meeting. The organizer had asked me to give a lunch talk about my recurrent themes: fossils are everywhere, fossils are really cool, fossils can be found by anyone, and small museums are important. The last thing I needed was another flight in a small regional jet, but I accepted the invitation because I saw that there was going to be a session about the Mammoth Site in Hot Springs, South Dakota. The organizer had asked me to moderate the session and introduce Larry Agenbroad, the godfather of the fossil site. I've been interested in this site since visiting it back in the 1993, and I had never met Larry, so I thought, why not?

Once I got there, I was happy that I had gone. Rapid City was enjoying an Indian summer, and the conference was small and friendly. The welcome basket in my hotel room had some awesome caramel corn and people laughed a lot at my lunchtime talk. I enjoyed listening to the latest science about the Mammoth Site and was delighted to have some quality time chatting with Larry. I had written about the Mammoth Site in my book, *Cruisin' the Fossil Freeway*, and I was curious about the relatively common occurrence of heavy-equipment operators discovering fossil sites. This happens often enough that I had been strategizing ways to be invited to national contractor meetings to talk about fossils, why they are so cool, and why contractors should not run in fear when they hear the word "paleontology."

After the symposium, Larry and I sat down, and he recounted the discovery of the mammoth site in 1974. A Hot Springs landowner, Phil Anderson, had hired a heavy-equipment operator named Porky Hansen to level some ground and prepare it for a building. Porky was pushing dirt when his blade ran across an odd white tusk-shaped object. Porky consulted Phil and they realized that it wasn't just tusk shaped—it was a tusk. Phil had a passing interest in paleontology, and he called around to see if any scientists were interested. Nobody returned his calls. He called some more people and they ignored his entreaties. He figured that mammoths must not be that interesting, so he decided that he might as well give it up and get Porky back to pushing dirt.

Larry Agenbroad, a paleontologist whom Phil hadn't called, had been

Every year, thousands of people come to Hot Springs, South Dakota, to see the Mammoth Site discovered by Porky Hansen.

digging fossils near Toadstool Park in western Nebraska when he heard about the discovery. He called Phil on a Sunday afternoon and said that he would come by and take a look. He did, and the tusk turned out to be attached to the skull. They dug and found more bones and more tusks, and today, 37 years after Porky's discovery, the site is visited by more than 100,000 tourists per year and is a significant boon to the economy of Hot Springs and the Black Hills region. Amazing science has been done, and the site has yielded the remains of 58 mammoths, most of them young males. It turns out that the animals had found themselves in a lake lined by slick clay walls, and they couldn't get out. It was a death trap for teen-aged males, a malicious mammoth mosh pit. I loved the story. I love mammoths. But what I really loved was Porky's name.

Two days later, my wife, Chase, and I flew to Seattle for a wedding on Camano Island in Puget Sound and to celebrate my dreaded 50th birthday. Chase had cooked up a surprise, but I could tell when we parked at the ferry landing that we were headed to see my oldest friend, Charlie, and his wife, Lucy, who lived in Port Townsend on the Strait of Juan de Fuca. Just because I knew where we were going, though, doesn't mean I knew what we were doing. When we landed at Port Townsend, we were met not only by Charlie and Lucy but also by my sister, from New York, and my dad, from Seattle. We drove down to the harbor and climbed aboard

Charlie and Lucy's 30-foot cabin cruiser and headed out into the dense fog and rain. You don't know me, but celebrating a big birthday by cruising around in the fog actually appeals.

It turned out that Charlie and Lucy had cooked up an outing to a quixotic destination. After a couple of hours, the fog gave way to high, flat, gray sky, and the water flattened down. An island loomed ahead, and Charlie started telling the curious tale of Protection Island. In 1965, the island was purchased by Seattle developers and subdivided into 800 lots. A number of people moved to the island and built homes. Over time, federal wildlife managers realized that the island was one of only a few tufted puffin and rhinoceros auklet nesting grounds south of Alaska. In 1982, Congress put the skids on the development, made the island into a national wildlife refuge, and started buying the property back from the lot owners. People were bought out on a sliding scale: the longer they stayed, the less they were paid for their property. Faced with the possibility of total loss, everyone sold—everyone except for a big lonely Indian named Marty Bluewater. Marty decided that living on the island was worth more than the money they would pay him for moving off of it, so he settled for a deal where he could stay until he died, and they wouldn't have to pay him a dime. The timing worked in Marty's favor, and he ended up being the only resident of a 379-acre island with a commanding view of Discovery Bay, the Olympic Mountains, and the Strait of Juan de Fuca.

It wasn't entirely clear to me how Charlie knew Marty, but when we pulled into the empty little harbor, Marty showed up in a rusty old van with a broken door and a damp old sofa in the back, and greeted Charlie and Lucy like they were his family. We all climbed in and drove up to Marty's house high on the top of the island. The weather had flattened to a perfect calm, and we could look down from our perch 300 feet above the sea directly into the clear saltwater and see harbor seals diving in search of snacks. Bald eagles floated in the sky. We had a great picnic, and Marty told us how he had come to be a modern-day Robinson Crusoe. It was a mellow and sweet way to spend a big-number birthday.

After lunch Marty showed us a magnificent mammoth tooth that he had picked up on the beach. It turns out that Protection Island is a big pile

Marty Bluewater looks south toward Puget Sound from his desolate island.

of ice age sand that washed off the huge lobe of glacial ice that gouged, then filled, what is now Puget Sound. Being a geologist, I knew what most Seattleites don't know, that a mere 21,000 years ago, Seattle was under a blanket of 3,000 feet of glacial ice. Marty's island was an ice age wash out. On Marty's walks along his beach, he would often find pieces of ice age mammals, and the most common finds were chunks of mammoth. My dad's teeth are getting old, and he tried to fit the giant mammoth molar in his mouth. Nothing doing; the tooth was the size of his head. Man, do I love mammoths.

I survived the party later that night and headed back to Denver to join my colleague and co-paleobotanist Ian Miller for an expedition to the Grand Staircase-Escalante National Monument in southern Utah. Ian and I had banded with the dinosaur paleontologists of the University of Utah to explore this amazing expanse of steep badlands in search of 75-million-year-old fossil plants. We had a great trip, and I learned a few things about Ian. I had known that he was a great scientist and a great guy. What I didn't know was that he was a superb logistics guy. He organized the expedition and coordinated food, equipment, supplies, camping gear, and people. We worked in an absurd landscape of nearly vertical mudstone, hiking down and then back up incredibly steep and dangerous slopes. The team cranked, and we found and collected amazing fossils. Nothing is more fun that digging fossils. But what really impressed me was how skilled Ian was at running a big field camp.

Just before Ian and I went to Utah, Kit Hamby, manager of the Snow-mass Water and Sanitation District, had started a long-awaited reservoir construction project at the top of Divide Road above Snowmass Village. A few miles from Aspen, Colorado, Snowmass Village is in an old ranching valley that turned into a ski resort back in 1967. Snowmass Village has four seasons: ski, mud, summer, and mud. During mud season, fewer than 2,800 people live in the town. During the peak of the ski season, more than 15,000 people crowd the condos and slopes, and the quiet town bursts into life.

Kit's biggest fear was that all 15,000 skiers would flush their toilets at the same time and the town would run out of water. That, and the fact that droughts happen, and fires happen, and people were building more and bigger homes, and a new base village was being planned, all added up to the town needing a place to store some spare water. Snowmass Village is in the Brush Creek Valley, but the town owns water rights on Snowmass Creek, in the next valley to the west. Normally Kit's workers take water from a ditch on East Snowmass Creek and route it through a pipe where the water runs downhill and into the water treatment plant.

On the divide between Snowmass Creek and Brush Creek, at the top of Divide Road, is a small 12-acre private lake owned by Doug Ziegler of West Bend, Wisconsin, and his extended family of six adult children. In 1958, Doug had taken a western vacation, discovered the property, and purchased it. Two years later, he hired a dozer operator to build a small earthen dam to create a lake, naming it after his daughter Deborah. A few decades later, when the Water and San District realized it needed more

Opposite left: Marty lives in a place where mammoth fossils are not uncommon. *Middle:* Kirk's dad, Dick Johnson, trying on a mammoth tooth for size. *Right:* A 75-million-year-old leaf from the mudstone mountains of southern Utah.

Above: Steep badlands of 75-million-year-old mudstone form "The Blues" in the Grand Staircase-Escalante National Monument in southern Utah. These rocks are full of dinosaurs, reptiles, mammals, and fossil plants.

storage, it set its sights on Lake Deborah. After years of negotiations, the district made a deal with Doug to buy the reservoir (but not the property around it), drain it, remove 80,000 yards of dirt, build a bigger dam, and create 250-acre feet of water storage for the town. They called it Ziegler Reservoir.

The negotiation was tough, and Doug had stipulated that the construction had to be done by the end of the 2011 construction season or the district would have to pay daily liquidated damages. Kit is a soft-spoken, competent man, and he knew that things had to go just right to finish his reservoir on time and avoid a costly outcome for his taxpayers.

Kit hired Gould Construction from Carbondale to remove the 80,000 yards of dirt to prepare the ground for the construction of an earthen dam. Work on the site began in September, shortly after I had headed to South Dakota. Kit hired an owner's representative for the project, Joe

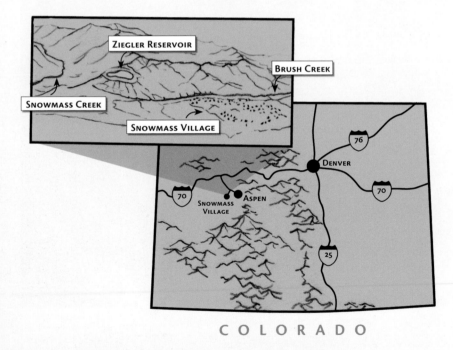

Ziegler Reservoir is located immediately west of Snowmass Village on the divide between Snowmass and Brush creeks.

Enzer, a mountain of a man who knows his business. Joe's job was to keep the project moving forward every day.

On September 20, the day after my birthday, Gould's crew began to push dirt. They were using D6 Cats and big track hoes, loading huge dump trucks to haul away the dirt. Work progressed smoothly, with the trucks making dozens of trips each day and creating an ever-deepening hole.

Kent Olson, Gould's on-site foreman, found a brown bone while walking across the site and had that odd feeling that contractors get when they find bones. He talked about the bone with his boss, Mark Gould, and they showed it to Bob Mutaw, an archaeologist who worked for URS, the engineering firm that was overseeing the site. Mutaw looked over the bone and pronounced it bovine, probably an old milk cow. Kent wasn't so sure.

The work continued, but the workers started making nervous jokes about old bones. Kent even played a practical joke by wrapping a big log in black plastic and sticking it on the tailgate of his project manager's truck. Then he casually mentioned that he had found a dinosaur bone. Not funny.

Gould's number-one dozer operator was Jesse Steele from Palisade, Colorado. Jesse is a polite, compact cowboy who wears a black hat and tips it when he greets a lady. He is also a third-generation dozer operator. As a toddler, he dozed in his grandfather's lap, in a dozer. He first drove a dozer at the age of five. When it comes to moving dirt, Jesse is a smooth operator.

At about four in the afternoon of October 14, Jesse was operating his D6, pushing through a thick brown layer of organic soil known as peat, when a pair of giant ribs flicked over the top of the blade. Jesse stopped the machine and hopped out to take a look. The ground in front of his blade was littered with big brown bones. Instead of getting excited, Jesse got scared.

Kent came over and together they began to gather the bones. They found a partial jawbone with an 8-inch-long tooth. They found a tusk. They found big vertebrae. It was clear that this was a big skeleton. Joe Enzer came over to the find, took one look, turned to Kent and said, "This is not a cow, and there is no way we can ever call it a cow." Kent took the bones home that night and got on the Internet. It didn't take him long to realize that Jesse had run over the skeleton of a mammoth.

This book is the story of what happened over the next nine months as Jesse's mammoth turned into the most significant high-elevation ice age fossil site in the world and the biggest fossil dig in Colorado history. I was in the right spot at the right time, my frustrating year suddenly got really interesting, and I was lucky to be the person to oversee the dig and write this story. In retrospect, the events of the previous month—my revisiting Porky's mammoth finds, Marty's mammoth birthday tooth, and Ian's big camps in the Grand Staircase-Escalante—all seemed to point to the fact that I didn't have to worry about life becoming boring once I turned 50. Instead, it was affirmed to me what I have known all along: there is nothing more fun than finding fossils.

Ian knows this too, and watching his team in the mudstone mountains of Utah convinced me that he should be the co-leader of the Snowmass project. He and I have collaborated on all aspects of this undertaking, and he has written the scientific sidebars in this book. We are both grateful to the more than 400 people who played a direct role in this vast and exciting effort.

Kirk Johnson
Denver, November 2011

Third-generation dozer operator
Jesse Steele, the hero of this story.

ACT ONE

It Starts with a Phone Call
FRIDAY, OCTOBER 15—WEDNESDAY, NOVEMBER 3, 2010

It was mid-morning on October 15. I was doing what I normally do in the morning, which is to spend hours that should be more productive engaged in the endlessly futile task of trying to tame the e-mail beast. Write a response and two more pop into the inbox. Is it work? I don't know, but I do it every day. A message on my voice mail was from Peter Barkmann of the Colorado Geological Survey. Someone had found a mammoth in Snowmass Village. They had called him, and he had called me.

I love getting those calls. The whole idea that the world is full of undiscovered fossils is such a happy one. The field of paleontology hasn't been around for that long and there have never been very many paleontologists. But there is a whole lot of ground out there, and that means that all the good stuff is waiting to be found. And I can tell you one thing: I'm not going to find fossils by answering e-mails. Finding fossils is like catching fish—if you want to catch a fish, you have to go fishing. If you want to find fossils, you have to go digging. And the reality is that the people doing most of the digging are not paleontologists, they are heavy-equipment operators like Porky and Jesse. The problem is that these guys are usually told by their foremen to ignore fossils and keep digging. It takes somebody to say, "Whoa, wait a minute, this might be cool. Maybe we should call someone."

It turns out that Jesse's discovery had already caused a lot of nervous conversation. Kent Olson had called his boss, Mark Gould. Joe Enzer had called his boss, Kit Hamby. And everyone was trying to understand what to do next. Mark Gould started thinking that since his company had been hired to haul the dirt away from the site, he owned that dirt. He did a little research on the web and discovered that mammoth skeletons are worth big dollars. Kit Hamby felt that it was his project and he needed to talk to his board to figure out the right thing to do. And he knew that he needed expert help.

After listening to the message, I went to find Ian. He was in a meeting. I yanked him out of the meeting. Something told me that we needed to move fast on this one. Ian assigned our new curator of geology, Whitey Hagadorn, to see what was going on, and Whitey spent a lot of the afternoon on the phone with Kit trying to understand the situation. From what he learned, there already seemed to be a lot of interest and concern about the find.

The next morning was a Saturday, and we sent Bryan Small, head of our fossil preparation lab, and two volunteers to Snowmass Village to see the bones and the site. After their visit, they drove home that night and reported that the bones were superbly preserved. This was looking like the real deal.

Word was getting out in the Roaring Fork Valley that something had been found, and people started coming to the Snowmass Water and Sanitation offices to see the bones. Excitement was starting to build.

On Monday, October 18, I assigned Ian to lead the project and started to think about how we should respond. I tried to get a hold of Steve Holen, our curator of archaeology and resident mammoth specialist, but as luck would have it, he had just left for a research trip to the Yukon that morning. Richard Stucky, our curator of fossil mammals, was enjoying a vacation in Egypt. I pondered Plan B for about 15 seconds, and then I called Dan Fisher.

CAST OF CHARACTERS

The dig at Snowmass Village fell together quickly between October 28 and November 4, 2010. Within those few days, people from several organizations came together to turn a construction site into a major fossil excavation. Meet some of the key players from the main organizations in this unfolding drama.

SNOWMASS WATER & SANITATION DISTRICT

Kit Hamby

Joe Enzer

URS CORP.

John Sikora

TOWN OF SNOWMASS VILLAGE

Bill Boineau

Russ Forrest

GOULD CONSTRUCTION

Mark Gould

Kent Olson

Jesse Steele

DENVER MUSEUM OF NATURE & SCIENCE

George Sparks

Kirk Johnson

Ian Miller

Richard Stucky

Steve Holen

Bryan Small

Cody Newton

Carol Lucking

Samantha Richards

Laura Holtman

Brendon Asher

Steve Nash

Dane Miller

Jude Southward

Jan Vriesen

Rick Wicker

Lisa Delonay

Liz Miller

U. S. GEOLOGICAL SURVEY

Jeff Pigati

Tom Ager

Paul Carrara

ADDITIONAL SCIENTISTS

Dan Fisher, University of Michigan

Greg McDonald, National Park Service

Russ Graham, Penn State University

SNOWMASS WATER & SANITATION DISTRICT

Water is our most precious resource, essential for the survival of all organisms on Earth. Yet 97.5 percent of all water on the planet is salty while only 2.5 percent is fresh. Of the freshwater, most of it, 98.7 percent, is trapped as ice at the North and South Poles or buried as groundwater deep below the planet's surface. All told, less than 1.3 percent of all freshwater is in snowfields, lakes, and rivers and is accessible to us to drink.

To ensure ample water year-round, communities form water districts to harness and manage their clean water resources. In the upper Roaring Fork Valley, the Snowmass Water and Sanitation District (SWSD) covers approximately 3,900 acres, including but not limited to the town of Snowmass Village. The district services 3,500 year-round residents and up to 16,000 residents during ski season through its water treatment plant, 12 storage tanks, and 44 miles of distribution pipelines.

In 2006, the district conducted a study that found that the community did not have enough raw water storage to support itself during a water crisis. They decided that they needed a reservoir. The district identified Doug Ziegler's lake above Snowmass Village as the best place to construct a reservoir because it is above the town and gravity could be used to distribute the water. It was already in a natural depression that could easily be enlarged by removing 80,000 cubic yards of sediment and building a taller earthen dam. SWSD would then fill the new reservoir by running water through a pipeline from East Snowmass Creek. In 2008, the district purchased the reservoir, and on September 20, 2010, it began construction. The district's goal was to expand the capacity of the reservoir from 50-acre feet to 250-acre feet (81 million gallons). Little did anyone know that by digging down into what turned out to be an ancient lake, the district would take the citizens of Colorado on a time machine back 130,000 years to see an amazing record of life in the ice age Rockies.

Dan, a professor at the University of Michigan, had started his scientific career studying ancient marine shells. But one day, a call had come into the geology department in Ann Arbor about a farmer who had found a big skeleton while draining a pond. Since he was the only person in the office, Dan went to investigate and ended up digging up a mastodon skeleton. That mastodon captured his imagination, and he never looked back. Over the years he dug up more mastodons, then mammoths, and in the process he became one of the top experts in the world.

I had come to know Dan while visiting a friend in Ann Arbor, and I found that I really liked him. For one, he was super nice and welcoming and thought there was nothing unusual about a paleobotanist coming by to chat about mastodons. For another, he was crazy smart and I was fascinated by how he used his brain to solve problems that other scientists didn't even know existed. I was a tourist in Dan's office that day, but over the years we developed a friendship, and in the fall of 2010, I realized that I should call him to get a better understanding of what we should do with the evolving Snowmass situation. To my delight, Dan was excited about the discovery and promised to help me figure it out.

The next day, Ian and his wife, Robyn, went to Snowmass to see the site. Things were starting to get complicated. Bob Mutaw, the archaeologist, wanted to dig the site and had rented a ground-penetrating radar device to see if he could image the bones in the ground. People continued to flood into the Snowmass Water and Sanitation District offices to see the bones. Kit was growing increasingly worried that his project was being derailed. Mark Gould was still wondering if it was possible to sell the bones.

Ian realized that not only was the site politically complicated, it was also geologically complicated. The skeleton was buried in a layer of fluffy organic peat, but there was also glacial till and layers of clay and silt in the lake bed, and the relationship between the layers wasn't so clear. That night, Ian had pizza with Bill Boineau, the bearlike mayor of Snowmass Village. In their conversation Ian learned that Bill not only

John Nicholl using ground-penetrating radar to seek evidence of more bones.

understood the potential of the site, but that he was also the son of the husband of my mom's college roommate. It turns out that Bill's stepsister is a paleontologist and a friend of mine. Only four months before, I had visited her at the La Brea Tar Pits in Los Angeles. I called Bill. We had our first political foothold.

The next morning, everything came to a head. Kit Hamby called an emergency open meeting of the Water and San board. The bones were there, the press was there, the public was there, and all of the stakeholders were there. The spotlight was on Ian. We conferred by phone, and decided to go for it. He proposed that the Denver Museum of Nature & Science would undertake the fossil portion of the excavation—and pay for it—as long as the Water and San board would donate the fossils to the museum.

Over the next weekend, more than a thousand people crowded through the Water and San office to see the bones. Snowmass Village cops spent the day doing traffic control. People began to wonder why the museum was doing the excavation and why they should give their fossils away. The Town of Snowmass Village started a Snowmass Mammoth Facebook page.

By October 26, it seemed like Kit Hamby was having second thoughts, and it looked like the deal might fall through. Steve Holen had returned

from the Yukon, and he, Ian, and I decided to go back to Snowmass to get the project back on track. The road over Vail Pass was icy and awful and I wondered what we were getting ourselves into, but I was also thinking about another thing that excited me more than icy roads scared me. I had just finished working with a team of scientists on a National Research Council report about the relevance of ancient climates to the discussion of global warming. One of our key conclusions was that it would be a very good thing to use ice age fossil sites to help the general public understand climate change. I wondered if Snowmass might not be that site that we were looking for.

We met with Kit and the water district's lawyer, Mark Hamilton, at the restaurant at the Snowmass Club. Clearly, Kit had been overwhelmed by the public interest in the site. He wanted to make sure that not only would we do the dig and pay for it, we would also promise to deliver educational programs to the Roaring Fork Valley and provide the town with a cast of the mammoth skeleton. We swallowed and agreed.

Left and below: Steve Holen inspects the bones of the discovery mammoth in the Snowmass Water and Sanitation District offices on October 27.

Then we went to look at the bones in the water district office. Within seconds, Steve realized that the mammoth was not a woolly mammoth but a Columbian mammoth. Then he spotted a bone from a larger mammoth. There were at least two animals.

Steve specializes in the study of ice age hunters—humans who killed and cooked mammoths, camels, and bison as recently as 13,000 years ago. There is an ongoing debate as to when humans first arrived in North America (estimates range from 13,800 to more than 30,000 years ago), and Steve is in the thick of this argument. For his whole career, he has been searching for evidence of the first Americans. Given the beautiful quality of the bones, he began to wonder out loud if the Snowmass site was a kill site where human hunters had butchered and eaten an animal. He found one bone that looked like it had been broken when it was still fresh. He started to get really excited. Ian and I joked about finding Snowmass Man.

We drove up to the site, which is just above Snowmass Village on a private road. The day was sunny, but it had recently snowed. Kit had erected a tent over the mammoth discovery site on the drained bed of the lake and had enclosed the tent within a chain-link fence. The rest of the site was abuzz with construction activity. We all were thinking that the mammoth was an isolated discovery.

I was dressed for speaking with lawyers, not for walking in the mud. I had expected to take a look in the tent and then head back for Denver. Twenty feet below us was a big hole, the site of the future dam, where a bulldozer was pushing dirt up an earthen ramp. The sun was causing the dirt to steam, and it looked like a scene from an icy hell. As we prepared to leave, Kent Olson from Gould Construction walked up to us holding a shard of a large bone. He said that it had come from the bottom of the hole.

Now there were three mammoths.

Ignoring the fact that we were wearing street clothes, we rushed down into the hole and started digging in the dirt with our bare hands. More shards of bone emerged from the moist gray silt. Soon Joe Enzer, Kent, Steve, Ian, and I were crawling in the dirt yelling for joy as we found huge chunks of bone. Jesse stayed in the cab of his D6 dozer. I found the tip of a tusk. Kent and Ian noticed that clear water would well up when the dozer hit a bone. Rhonda Bazil from the Water and San board joined us, and soon she too was squealing with delight as she pulled bones from the

Left: Steve Holen, Kent Olson, Kit Hamby, and Joe Enzer ponder the discovery of new bones on October 27. *Above:* Steve Holen holds the broken end of a mastodon humerus. At the time, we thought it was a mammoth bone.

ground. We were gradually engulfed with the realization that this was not just a solitary mammoth but a very significant high-elevation ice age site. We groveled in the dirt until the sun set, then we drove home to Denver dirty but excited.

That night, I didn't sleep much. My mind was racing. I was pumped. It is a pretty cool feeling to be present at the beginning of major discovery and to know it. I knew that this find had the potential to be huge, and I decided that I was going to drop everything and make it happen. I could tell that it was going to be a complicated project, so I decided that I would move to Snowmass for the duration to ensure that my team had the support they would need to pull off the dig.

The next morning, I met with museum CEO George Sparks and the museum's other vice presidents. They were excited, and their response was really positive. I walked out of the room with their support to undertake a significant excavation. At the time, we were thinking that this effort might cost as much as $40,000 dollars. Man, were we wrong.

Then, I rallied my troops. As chief curator of the fourth largest natural history museum in the country, I have lots of help when it comes to delivering the museum's mission of making scientific discoveries, preserving the objects, and sharing the discoveries with the public. I crammed paleontologists, archaeologists, collection managers, research assistants, conservators, registrars, preparators, educators, and exhibit developers into my office and told them that we were about to launch a major excavation. Then we spent the rest of the morning figuring out what that meant, who would

Left: Museum staff gathered in Kirk's office on the morning of October 28. *Right:* John Sikora holding the first mastodon tooth.

be involved, and what we needed to do next. While we were talking, Steve Holen received an image on his cell phone. Joe Enzer had just discovered a mastodon tooth.

Mammoths and mastodons lived at the same time but not typically in the same place. Mastodons are forest browsers, while mammoths are plains grazers. Yet at Snowmass we had the teeth and bones of both. Although there had been more than 100 previous mammoth discoveries in Colorado, there had been only three previous mastodon discoveries in the state's history. In less than 12 hours, the site had already exceeded my expectations, and I decided that we needed to deploy the team immediately. I told Steve to grab a crew and return to Snowmass that afternoon.

By coincidence, the museum was hosting the Jackson Hole Film Festival, and the president of National Geographic Television had been in attendance. We called his cell phone and caught him on the way to the airport. He said that they were interested in the project. Later that day we had a conference call with National Geographic and made a verbal agreement to work exclusively with them to make a documentary about the discovery.

By noon on October 29, Steve Holen and the advance party were back on site, and bones were everywhere. Gould's heavy-equipment operators were still removing dirt, and fossils were appearing across the expanse of the big hole. The heavy-equipment operators had found three big, beautiful intact tusks and one that lay shattered in the ground. By the end of the day, Steve thought he had evidence of nine different animals, but it wasn't clear how many were mammoths, and how many were mastodons.

That same afternoon, and after multiple lawyerly conversations, the museum signed the agreement with SWSD that allowed us to undertake the dig. It turned out that the SWSD did not own the fossils on its property, nor did they have the legal right to donate them to the museum. Since SWSD is a taxing

entity in the state of Colorado, the state owns the fossils. And that meant that we had to obtain an excavation permit from the Colorado state archaeologist. That permit came through on October 29, and we were finally ready to begin the dig, along with help from Gould Construction, whose crews would also continue work on the reservoir project.

For the next two days, Steve and his team worked to stabilize the broken tusk and encase it in strips of burlap soaked in plaster of paris. Since he was working with a small crew, Steve turned our museum educator, Samantha Richards, into a digger. When I called Samantha for a progress report, she told me that she was "cold, muddy, and plastered." She sounded utterly delighted.

Steve inspected the discovery mammoth and decided that we should do a controlled archaeological-style excavation of it using a measured grid. Without knowing the age of the fossil, it was not possible to know if the animal had been killed by human hunters, and Steve wanted to make sure that we proceeded with the utmost caution so that we would not

Joe Enzer, Kent Olson, and Jesse Steele with three mastodon tusks on the morning of October 28.

This mastodon skeleton was collected in a bog in Indiana in 1932 before being acquired by the Colorado Museum of Natural History (now DMNS) in 1935. Mastodons are more heavily built than mammoths and tend to have straighter tusks. They are browsing animals that lived in areas with lots of trees. Before the Snowmass discovery, there were only three mastodon finds in Colorado history. The last mammoths and mastodons lived in North America around 13,000 years ago.

The Angus mammoth was first mounted at the Colorado Museum of Natural History (now DMNS) in 1932. This 75,000-year-old skeleton was collected near Angus, Nebraska, before being sold to the museum in Denver. The 13-foot-tall skeleton was nearly complete, but the head was missing and had to be fabricated. Mammoths are taller than mastodons and are grazing animals that lived in areas with lots of grass. There have been more than 100 mammoth finds in Colorado history. The museum staff includes the museum's first paleontologist, Philip Reinheimer (far left), and its first director, Jesse Dade Figgins (second from left).

HOW RADIOCARBON DATING WORKS

Learning the age of a fossil is critical for understanding its place in prehistory. There are many techniques for discovering the age of fossils, but the most precise are based on radioactive decay. All matter is made up of elements, which are made of atoms, which in turn are made of particles called protons, electrons, and neutrons. Elements come in many different flavors, determined by their number of neutrons. These flavors are called isotopes. Carbon has three different isotopes: C-12, C-13, and C-14. Some isotopes are stable and nonreactive (C-12 and C-13); others are unstable and radioactive (C-14). Unstable isotopes eventually break down into stable isotopes in a process that emits radiation, called radioactive decay. What makes this process so special to paleontologists is that the radioactive decay is constant and measurable.

One common type of radioactive decay dating is radiocarbon dating. Carbon is a ubiquitous element. It is in the air we breathe, the food we eat, and in all the plants and animals we see around us. Most carbon is stable, but in the atmosphere some carbon atoms become radioactive as they are bombarded by cosmic rays from outer space. This small amount of radioactive carbon, along with lots of stable carbon, is incorporated in living plants during photosynthesis. Animals, including humans,

eat those plants, and the radioactive carbon becomes part of our bodies. Since the amount of radioactive carbon in the atmosphere varies very little, we know how much radioactive carbon is in plants and animals when they are alive. When they die and stop actively acquiring carbon, the radioactive carbon decays and becomes less common relative to the stable carbon isotopes. For carbon, half of all the radioactive isotopes decay to stable isotopes in 5,730 years. This is called the half-life of radioactive carbon. After two half-lives, or 11,460 years, half again has decayed and now only one-quarter of the radiocarbon is left. In a fossil, whether plant or animal, we can measure the amount of radiocarbon in the specimen and use it to tell how many half-lives have elapsed and thus determine its age. If 50 percent is left, then one half-life, or 5,730 years, have elapsed and the fossil is 5,730 years old; if 25 percent is left, then two half-lives have elapsed and it is 11,460 years old. After eight half-lives, or 45,840 years, only 0.4 percent of the radioactive carbon is left and it becomes too hard to measure. Fossils older than about 45,000 years are considered radiocarbon dead because too little radiocarbon is left to date them using this technique.

So, as useful as radiocarbon dating is, most of the Snowmass site was radiocarbon dead, implying that most of the events at the site occurred before 45,000 years ago.

The fossil wood at Ziegler Reservoir looks like last year's driftwood, but it contains no measurable radioactive carbon. This means that it is actually more than 45,000 years old.

destroy any evidence of human presence. He also took samples of the peat for radiocarbon dating, to try to determine the age of the animal. While Steve and the crew were assessing the site, Laura Holtman, our public relations representative, worked with Kit to arrange a schedule for the bones to begin visiting schools from Aspen down the valley to Rifle.

On November 1, museum CEO George Sparks arrived on the site and helped the crew prepare to begin major excavation the following day. Steve Holen shipped the radiocarbon samples to a company that promised a five-day turnaround. Ian had been shopping for supplies all weekend and arrived in Snowmass around seven in the evening with nine diggers. The official dig was poised to start the next morning.

On the morning of November 3, George returned to Denver with five tusks packed in his car. That afternoon, he and I drove back to Snowmass. We stopped for dinner in Glenwood Springs and met with Mark Gould. We were thinking about how we would pay for the excavation, and we figured that because of his business connections, Mark might help us understand how to go about raising funds in the Roaring Fork Valley.

We finally got to Snowmass Village around nine o'clock. The previous week, Ian had met Dave Spence, the former head of the Water and San board and manager of Top of the Village Condominiums. Since it was mud season, Ian had been able to negotiate a great price for roomy, slope-side ski condos. When George and I arrived, our accommodations suggested that we were on vacation rather than on a dig.

By this time our team had grown to about 25 people, all booked in luxury condominiums as well. That took care of lodging. As for food, that's where our secret weapon, Ian's mom, Liz Miller, came into play. Ian comes from a family of five brothers, so Liz has been den mother in charge of the pack of giant men-children for 30 years. Liz was planning to spend the winter working at a scientific research station in Antarctica, but when Ian told her about the discovery, she canceled her plans and joined the team. Over the next two weeks, Liz would cook breakfast, lunch, and dinner for the entire crew.

Cross section of Ziegler Reservoir, looking south, showing how it is located on top of the ridge between Snowmass Village and Snowmass Creek.

Luxury Digs
THURSDAY, NOVEMBER 4–WEDNESDAY, NOVEMBER 10, 2010

On November 4, 21 days after Jesse's initial discovery, we had a full team on site. And what a curious site it was. As a geologist, one of the first things I do when I visit a new place is to try to understand how the place came to be. I observe the bedrock, scan the topography, and try to construct a historical narrative in my head about how the landscape of the place had evolved.

The modern lake had been drained back in the summer, so we were confronted with a 12-acre circle of mud surrounded by an aspen-covered ridge. When Doug Ziegler bought the property in 1958, the future site of Lake Deborah was a bowl-shaped meadow that was popular with local sheepherders. In 1961, Doug hired local dozer operator Johnny Hyrup to build a 12-foot-high earthen dam so he could have a lake and stock it with fish. The dam worked and Doug got his lake, but the shallow lake froze out the fish each winter, and Doug eventually gave up on fishing there.

With some simple observations of Gould's excavation, I was quickly able to deduce that Doug's 1961 lake was located on top of the filled remains of an ancient glacial lake that had formed inside a circular ridge known as a glacial moraine. The moraine ridge had been created by a river of ice

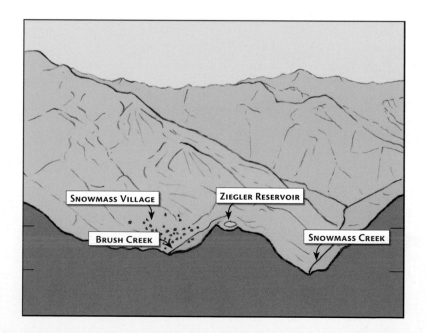

SNOWMASS VILLAGE
ZIEGLER RESERVOIR
BRUSH CREEK
SNOWMASS CREEK

(glacier) flowing down the adjacent Snowmass Creek Valley and grinding away at the valley walls as it went. The detritus from all of this grinding was a porridge of unsorted clay, sand, gravel, and boulders that lay on top of, and at the margins of, the ice. Once the glacier melted away, the sloppy boulder mess consolidated into a moraine. For a geologist, a moraine is a precise marker of where the glacier once was. Because there was a bowl of glacial moraine on the ridge top, I knew that the glacier had overtopped its valley.

Outside the circular moraine ridge, it was downhill in all directions: downhill to Snowmass Creek on the west, downhill to Wildcat Ridge on the north, downhill to Brush Creek and Snowmass Village to the east, and downhill to Divide Road to the south. Lakes are usually at the bottoms of hills, not the top. This was an unusual lake. Because the lake filled most of the bowl, the remaining catchment was small enough that no streams flowed into the lake, and the confining walls meant that no streams flowed out of it either. This meant that the lake filled only by precipitation and emptied only by

Above: Doug and Scott Ziegler in 1960 on the sheep meadow that would become Lake Deborah and then Ziegler Reservoir. *Below:* Bluffs of Mancos Shale stand above Snowmass Village. This gray, crumbly rock was the bottom of a muddy seafloor 80 million years ago.

evaporation. It is the fate of most lakes to fill up with river-borne sediment and eventually become marshes and then solid ground. This lake had filled up all right, but instead of filling with stream-borne sand and mud, it had filled with wind-borne silt, a rare situation indeed.

The circular ridge of moraine sits on top of gray shale that forms the bedrock of Snowmass Village. This gray rock is 80-million-year-old marine mud called Mancos Shale. Back in 1966, the Denver Museum of Nature & Science got a call from a couple of kids who had been out hunting with their dad near Old Snowmass. They had been working their way up a dry gully floored by gray shale when they came upon a massive rib cage. A team from the museum arrived the next summer to inspect the find. It turned out to be an amazing and complete 13-foot-long fish skeleton, a monstrous beast with huge teeth, called *Xiphactinus*. That fish was excavated and taken back to Denver to be stored in one of our many collection vaults.

To add some time perspective, when the Mancos Shale was slowly accumulating at the bottom of a shallow, salty sea, very little of Colorado was above sea level and the Rocky Mountains had yet to form. Eventually, forces within the earth pushed up the Rocky Mountains and the forces of water and ice erosion carved and shaped the drainages of the Roaring Fork Valley. Understanding this site would demand that we understand the details of this geologic history.

Above: The 13-foot-long, 80-million-year-old *Xiphactinus* fish from the Mancos Shale near Old Snowmass. *Left:* Denver museum staff collecting the fish skeleton in 1967.

of us scattered around the site trying to understand how the fossils were distributed in the sediments. Half the crew worked on the top of the pile looking for bones, leaves, and cones in the peat that contained the remains of the discovery mammoth. The other half worked down in the hole where the bones, teeth, and tusks of mastodons had been found.

Finding fossils is all about finding the layers of sediment or sedimentary rock that contain the fossils. I always say that it's really easy to find fossils if you can find the matrix that they are in. We had only begun to figure this site out. We knew that there was a 5-foot layer of clay on top of a 5-foot layer of peat on top of a 15-foot layer of silt on top of a glacial moraine. At least that is what the diagrams produced by the engineer for the construction project showed. They had drilled a dozen holes to see the layers and guide their design for the reservoir. At first it seemed that we had mammoth fossils in the peat and mastodon fossils at the very top of the moraine.

To know more, we needed to dig more. Two dozers were pushing dirt, and we had people walking alongside them watching to see if they would clip a bone with the big blades. There was about 6 feet between the blade and the tracks, and if you could alert the operator quickly enough, he wouldn't

Brendon Asher (left) and Steve Nash, chair of the museum's anthropology department, begin the excavation for the remainder of the discovery mammoth.

run over the fossil with the tracks. We called the people who walked alongside the dozers "blade runners."

Dane Miller, Ian's brother and one of our chief volunteers, was an ace blade runner. He quickly developed a rapport with Jesse, and it was amazing to watch them work together. Not only was Dane great at seeing the bones as they appeared between the blade and the track, but Jesse also had a remarkable touch with the blade. He would often feel something with the blade and stop the machine before Dane actually saw the bone. We were all amazed that Jesse could tell the difference between bone,

For the moment, we focused on the hole in front of us. The approach road from Divide Road reached the lake at its eastern edge, the site of the past and future dam. Gould Construction had been charged with clearing the dam site by removing the 25 feet of silt, clay, and peat that covered the glacial moraine. The top of the glacial moraine would be the foundation for the new earthen dam. The elevation of the water in the completed reservoir would be 8,875 feet above sea level. The discovery mammoth had been found in the peat layer below the floor of the drained lake at an elevation of 8,855 feet. The hole between the access road and the site of the discovery mammoth was pretty deep. Parts of it were as low as 8,840 feet. It was in this deep hole that Gould needed to remove sediment to find the top of the moraine, and it was in this sediment that we were finding mastodon bones.

Steve Holen and two of his contract archaeologists, Cody Newton and Brendon Asher, set about excavating the discovery mammoth. The rest wood, and rock simply by how the blade scraped against it. I've always liked digging and have been drawn to digging with bigger and bigger tools. Here, we were literally digging fossils with a bulldozer.

Back in the tent, it was a different story. Kit had erected the tent where Jesse had dozed the skeleton, but they had picked up all the pieces so it was not immediately clear that there were any fossils left to dig up. Steve Holen was really concerned that the site might include some evidence that humans were responsible for the demise of the animal, so he instructed Cody and Brendon to lay out a 1-meter string grid and dig the site in careful archaeological style. They arranged the grid to cover a large area along the north half of the tent in a shallow trench that Kit said was the mark of a dozer push that had yielded all the bones. Watching these guys work was incredible. They patiently set up the grid and then began to slowly scrape out 1-square-meter "units." They worked methodically and slowly, using trowels and brushes.

Soon, the 1-meter units began to grow down into the peat, and as the imposed geometry emerged, the site started to look like a large piece of brown graph paper. For a while, they dug in pure brown peat with not a bone to be seen. The peat itself was pretty incredible: soft, fluffy, and composed of pure organics. Some pieces held springy strands of sphagnum moss. Other pieces had linguine-like leaves of ancient sedges that were transparent, yellow, and flexible. Amazingly,

Above: Dane Miller running blade on Jesse's D6. *Left:* The peat from Ziegler Reservoir is so well preserved that plant parts peel right off and are still flexible. *Right:* Ziegler Reservoir construction site on November 4.

some were even green when they were exhumed. These leaves oxidized to brown or yellow within minutes.

It seemed like an act of faith to carve these perfectly square holes into the peat, but within a few hours, beautiful brown bones began to appear in the bottom of the pits. Kit's instincts had been right—there was more of the skeleton to be had. Our volunteers worked with a curious mixture of excitement and patience.

As much I wanted to join them, I needed to make sure that we were really welcome in the valley. George and I drove down to the Snowmass

The delicate leg bones of the deer survived being run over by the D6 dozer.

Club for a lunch with Kit Hamby, Town Manager Russ Forrest, and Susan Hamley from Snowmass Tourism. Already, the town was beginning to understand how important this site could be for them. Over my 30 years as a paleontologist, I had watched fossil discoveries make an economic impact on small towns, and I was really curious to see if this discovery could do something for Snowmass Village.

I was just starting to eat when I got a text message saying that the team had discovered two animals in the peat, a small deer-like animal and part of a bison. History was happening and I was eating salad. Then, Mike Kaplan, CEO of the Aspen Skiing Company, walked by and we chatted about his company's progressive stance on global warming and how this discovery might be significant for them as well.

After lunch we rushed back to the site. The deer-like animal had been run over by the dozer. Bambi meets Godzilla all over again. The guys had found a few small bones in the push pile and had traced them back to where a graceful little leg bone was protruding from the peat. An inch-long toe bone was clearly visible. We placed a bunch of little flags around the bones and kept looking.

Down in the hole, one of our volunteers, Lorie Mihelich,

had uncovered a really unusual bone that was about 2 feet long. It was as thick as a baseball bat, but it had a wide, flat flange at one end. Richard Stucky, our curator of fossil mammals, had just left the site to return to Denver, and was walking to his car. I sent someone to go get him and bring him back.

Paleontologists play a fun game when they find a fossil bone. The first question is: What bone in the body is it? Is it a rib, pelvis, a thigh bone, or a vertebra? Once they have identified the type of bone, they then ask: Which species was it? You might think that this is easy, but there are more than 5,000 species of living mammals in the world, so recognizing one from a single bone is not that easy. Combine that with the fact that there are lots of extinct species in the fossil record, and you start to see how fun this game can be.

I was puzzled by the bone and didn't even recognize what part of the body it came from. Someone suggested it was a humerus (upper arm bone). Then I remembered an old paleontological adage: If an ice age bone looks really odd, it might be a giant ground sloth. Armed with these two ideas, I took out my iPhone and googled "giant ground sloth humerus." Much to my amazement, the first picture that came up on the screen was identical to the bone that was lying in the dirt at my feet. We had found a giant ground sloth. Just then Richard came down the hill and confirmed the identification.

By the end of the first full day, we had bones from five big mammals: mammoth, mastodon, bison, something deer-like, and

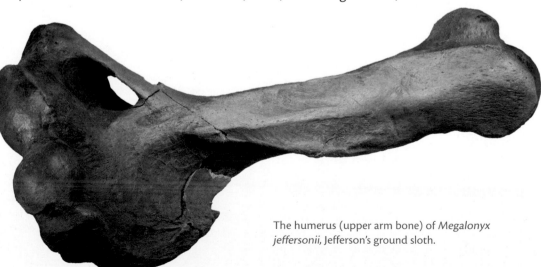

The humerus (upper arm bone) of *Megalonyx jeffersonii*, Jefferson's ground sloth.

giant ground sloth. Things were moving really fast, and I was relieved when Dan Fisher arrived from Michigan that evening. The fossils were appearing rapidly and, fortunately, so were the paleontologists. We planned to hold a press conference the next morning to get the word out, and the public relations team from the museum came to Snowmass to support the effort.

The morning of November 5 was cold and sunny. I drove down to the base of the valley to shoot a photo of the village for the press conference. We held the event in the partially constructed Base Village, a huge new facility at the base of the ski slope. The recent recession had halted construction and thrown the project into foreclosure, so we were the only people there and the site had the feel of a modern high-end ghost town. In contrast, the room where we held the press conference was warm and welcoming. More than 100 people assembled, and a real buzz of excitement was in the air. Clearly, we were not the only people to think that this discovery was a big deal. Steve, Ian, and I all spoke, as did Kit and the mayor. For the first time, it seemed like we were really working as a team.

After lunch we returned to the site. The sun had come out and things looked fine, but something seemed amiss. At first I couldn't place it, but eventually I noticed that the dozers seemed to be moving faster than the day before. I wandered over to the edge of the big hole and peered in. Two dozers were pushing dirt side by side. They were flanked by blade

runners, but they were moving really fast. Two track hoes were loading dirt in dump trucks, and they were also cranking. One of the track hoes was a whopper with a huge bucket. Mark Gould himself was operating the big beast, and a big cylinder of concrete was swinging by a chain from the bucket. It seemed like things were moving too fast, but what did I know about excavation? Dane and my research assistant Carol Lucking, who were blade-running, seemed pretty agitated. Carol told me,

"It's a good thing my mother doesn't know what I'm doing."

I wandered out of the pit and climbed up onto the slope to the north to get a bigger picture of the site. Just then, a little black helicopter flew into view and began to land over on the west side of the site. As it got close to the ground, it blew up a huge cloud of dust. I could see that a videographer whom we had hired to document the dig was walking over to the helicopter and starting to get in. Just then I spotted Joe Enzer running toward the chopper. His face was the color of a beet, and he was screaming. As he got close, the videographer backed away and the chopper took off, leaving a red-faced Joe awash in a plume of dust. All of this made no sense to me.

I ran down to the haul road where the dust had settled, but the tension remained thick. Joe was yelling at Mark. Kit arrived. Then the Snowmass police arrived. And then Pitkin County sheriff's deputies showed up. The cops were sporting blue jeans and John Denver haircuts. They reminded me of *Starsky and Hutch* (the original series, not the remake). In our brief

Left: Two dozers and one track hoe are a lot for one blade runner to keep up with. *Above:* None of us understood why this helicopter pilot chose to drop by for a visit.

absence at the press conference, the site had spun out of control.

Eventually the cops left, everyone cooled down, and we pieced together what had happened. Gould's foreman Kent and been called away to attend a funeral, leaving the equipment operators unsupervised. The helicopter pilot had met the videographer in a bar the night before, and he had offered to take her up for some aerial photographs. The pilot had called Mark's cell phone for permission to land, but Mark was busy operating the track hoe and never heard the phone ring. Mark, meanwhile, had been pushing his guys to finish the excavation before snowfall ended the excavation season. We had focused on the press conference and left our less experienced crew to run blade. No harm was done, but we learned a lesson. From that point on, Ian and I agreed that one of us would be on site at all times.

That night, two more scientists arrived. Russ Graham from Penn State, an expert on the distribution of ice age animals in North America, also studies the forensics of fossil sites to understand their ecology. Greg McDonald from the National Park Service is a giant ground sloth expert. Greg was delighted to hear about the sloth humerus and quickly identified the animal as *Megalonyx jeffersonii*, or Jefferson's ground sloth. This animal was originally described by none other than Thomas Jefferson, our first and only paleontologist president. Jefferson had received fossil bones from a place called Big Bone Lick in Kentucky. Because giant ground sloths have big claws, Jefferson mistakenly thought that he was looking at a giant predatory cat. Part of his impetus to launch the Lewis and Clark expedition came from his thought that such animals might be found alive in the wild, western portions of North America. The discovery of complete giant ground sloth fossils in South America a few years later corrected this mistake, and the animal was named for Jefferson. Although paleontologists had recorded parts of nine

JEFFERSON'S GROUND SLOTH
Megalonyx jeffersonii

different examples of Harlan's ground sloth in Colorado, the Snowmass sloth was the first example of *Megalonyx* in Colorado and the highest-elevation example found anywhere. Greg knew that in other parts of the country, *Megalonyx* were often found in association with mastodons, suggesting that they shared a preference for certain types of ecosystems.

The tradition of evening recaps began that night. During recap, each of the scientists recounted what he or she had learned during the day and floated new hypotheses for what we were seeing. This turned out to be a very popular way for the team to learn about the discoveries of the day, to see how science happens, and to receive their assignments for the next day. It also made for some great stand-up comedy. Unfortunately, it turned out that Greg was such an endless source of awful sloth puns that groans exceeded laughs the nights that he was there.

On November 6, Bruce Bartleson, a geologist from Western State College in Gunnison, arrived on the site along with Peter and Cathy Dea. Peter, a geologist, was also the president of the museum's board of trustees. We continued our discussion about the formation of the site and debated how and when this glacial lake had formed and how

Dan Fisher holds court at the evening recap. This is where the crew reported on the day's discoveries.

long it had lasted. We were still waiting for the results from the radiocarbon samples that we had sent to Florida, and we were all still operating under the assumption that the quality of preservation suggested that the site couldn't be much older than 13,000 years.

We now had a pretty big crew of scientists and volunteers on site and were focusing our efforts on excavating the mammoth under the tent. We had smaller crews digging down in the hole where the mastodon and sloth bones had been found. We were in general agreement that the silt layer between the moraine and the peat was barren of fossils. Mark Gould, who had supervised the excavation of nearly 80,000 yards of sediment over the previous month, was convinced that his guys had seen no bones in the silt.

Early in the afternoon, this conviction was changed by a dramatic event. Jesse was slowly pushing his dozer through the silt layer at the bottom of the hole with Dane and Ian running blade. Just below the tent, the dozer unearthed a 3-foot-long bone that initially looked like another tusk. Upon close inspection, we realized that the bone was the core of an absolutely immense bison horn. It had been broken into three pieces and there were fresh breaks, indicating that the horn had been sheared from a skull. The pieces exposed the center of the horn, which was formed of a coarse, butterscotch-colored honeycomb latticework. It looked good enough to eat.

We stopped the dozer and spread out with shovels, trying to find the

Left: Dan Fisher digging around the bison skull.
Right: Steve Holen is dwarfed by the giant ice age bison.

skull. Eight of us looked for the better part of two hours with absolutely no luck. Finally we gave up, grudgingly deciding that the horn must have been a solitary fragment. With that decision, we asked Jesse to fire up the dozer and take another next pass. Amazingly, this time the dozer pushed up a second immense horn. And this time we were able find the spot in the silt where the horn had come from. After an hour of shoveling, we uncovered an incredibly large skull. Both horns fit back to the skull, and we came face-to-face with a huge bison. Productivity dropped way down as the entire crew gathered around to watch the beast emerge from the silt.

We carefully wrapped the two horns and applied burlap and plaster to the giant skull. It was hard to tell that day, but when measured, the skull was an amazing 6 feet 4 inches from broken horn tip to broken horn tip.

The bison discovery prompted volunteers Bill and Judy Peterson to hand me a $100 bill, the first financial contribution to the project. It also profoundly affected Cathy Dea, who had helped to encase the skull in plaster and in the process had coated herself in plaster and mud. She looked like a muddy urchin, but the look on her face was one of rapturous delight. A good fossil can do that to you.

For Russ Graham, an expert in ice age bison, this big beast rang some bells. Based on his knowledge, the big-horned bison went extinct more than 40,000 years ago. Russ suggested that our idea that the site was only 13,000 years old was probably wrong. While waiting for the radiocarbon dates to come back in a few days, people started to make wagers about the age of the site.

That night at recap, Peter Dea, Bruce Bartleson, Russ Graham, and I pored over a geologic map of the area that had been published in 1972 by USGS geologist Bruce Bryant. It was pretty clear from his

MAPPING ICE AGE MAMMALS

If you know where and how to look, fossils are everywhere. They are found in road cuts, construction sites, mountainsides, and stream banks. For example, the Denver Museum of Nature & Science houses plant and animal fossils from more than 500 sites in the greater Denver area alone. A Denver man even found a partial skeleton of a *Tyrannosaurus rex* during the construction of his neighbor's house. Expand to all of North America and there are tens of thousands of fossil sites dotting our continent.

Typically, paleontologists have focused on studying only a few of these sites at once. In this way, we have learned a tremendous amount about particular animals or plants and their local ecosystems. But what if you could study all the fossil sites at once? You could ask and answer questions about the interaction of ecosystems on the scale of the continent, tell if a major extinction happened all at once or in patches, and gauge where big-range animals like mammoths and mastodons roamed in North America. Drs. Russell Graham at Penn State and Ernest Lundelius from the University of Texas at Austin did just that.

Russ and Ernie developed FAUNMAP, an electronic database documenting the distribution of mammal species in North America over the last 5 million years. Their goal was to mine the scientific literature for fossil sites with mammals and record the mammals, location, age, cultural associations, and depositional environment of each site, then use that data to address basic ecological questions. FAUNMAP has been used to understand how mammals have responded to shifting climate, how their ranges have changed, and whether there are fundamental differences in past ecosystems compared to present-day ecosystems.

Anyone can use the FAUNMAP database (www.ucmp.berkeley.edu/faunmap/). It has an easy-to-use mapping interface similar to Google Maps. You can use it to discover fossils in your backyard or to investigate your own questions about the Pleistocene and beyond.

Russ Graham holds a mammoth tooth.

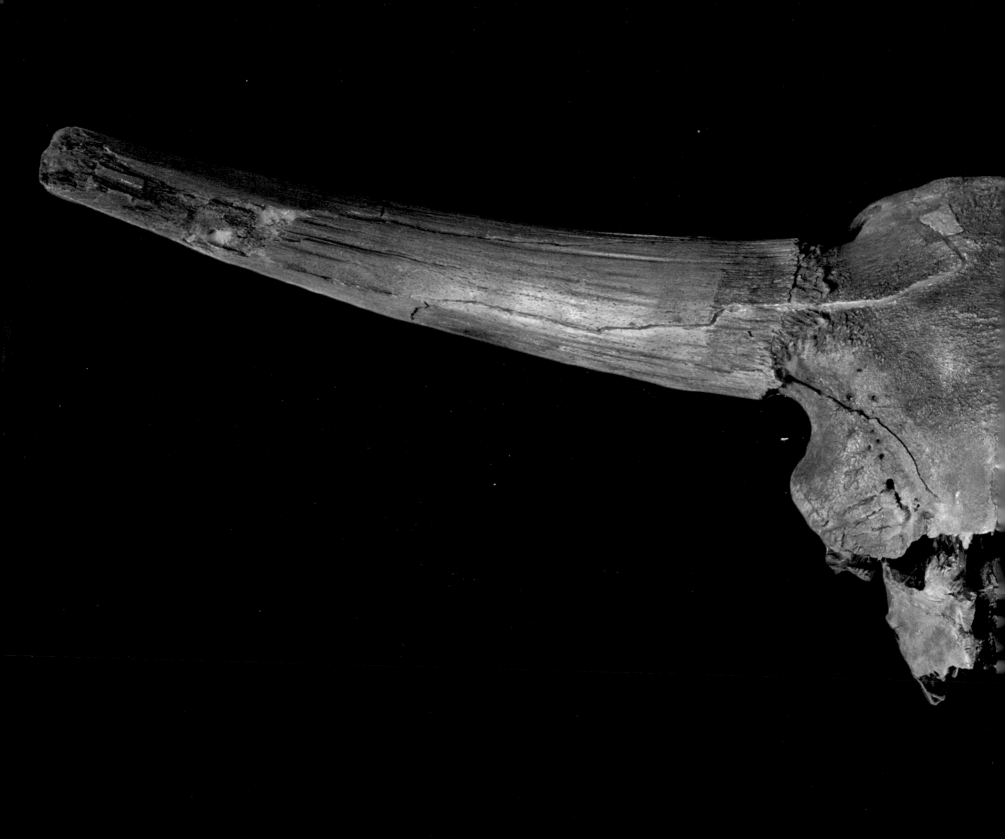

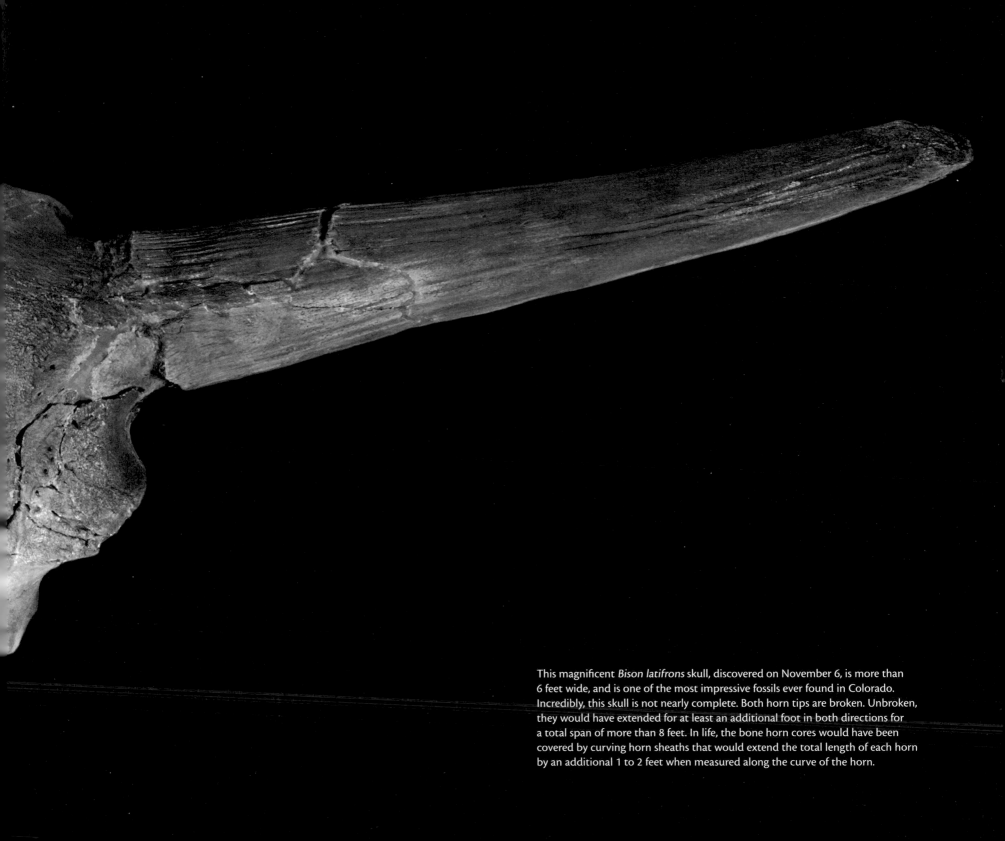

This magnificent *Bison latifrons* skull, discovered on November 6, is more than 6 feet wide, and is one of the most impressive fossils ever found in Colorado. Incredibly, this skull is not nearly complete. Both horn tips are broken. Unbroken, they would have extended for at least an additional foot in both directions for a total span of more than 8 feet. In life, the bone horn cores would have been covered by curving horn sheaths that would extend the total length of each horn by an additional 1 to 2 feet when measured along the curve of the horn.

Ian's Day:
ON THE GROUND AT ZIEGLER RESERVOIR

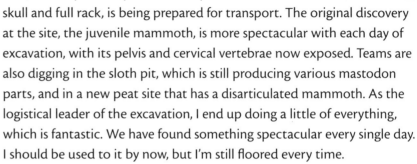

Saturday, November 6, 5:45 a.m. BEEP, BEEP, BEEP. Oh, man ... I can't believe it's already time to crawl out of bed. Feels like my head just hit the pillow. "Sit up before you pass out again," I tell myself. Five hours of sleep; not too bad, actually. Better than the night before.

Coffee. I need coffee. I smell it brewing already. Even better, I hear the unmistakable sound of sizzling bacon. Mom's cooking. Now I'm starting to perk up. My brother, still snoring, apparently didn't hear the alarm. "Up time!" I bawl. Dane "Dozer" Miller rolls over, not amused. He's still wearing his mud-covered shirt from yesterday. "Dude, let's go. We've got mammoths to find!"

Five minutes later, coffee in hand, we're in the kitchen helping our mom, Liz Miller, cook breakfast for 42 people before heading out to the Ziegler Reservoir site in Snowmass Village.

Paleontology for the Millers has always been a family affair. Nothing quite passes the time like cracking rocks and finding fossils with my four brothers. Dane and Mom are here because I know they rule when it comes to organizing a paleo dig. Some combination of the Miller family has led many successful trips to Cretaceous locales throughout the American West.

We arrive on-site at 6:45 a.m. It's freezing, literally, and still dark. We want to make sure we're there when the bulldozers are fired up for the day. We watch every pass of the blade to catch a mastodon femur or some other priceless Pleistocene cache. Dane has proven exceptional at this task. He's found more ribs, teeth, and tusks than anyone while running 10 hours a day in knee-deep mud, 3 feet from an 18-ton bulldozer. Dozer Dane leads the blade runners.

By 7 a.m., the dozers roll. More crew members arrive and deploy to four dig sites. The fossil deer, an exceptional specimen complete with a skull and full rack, is being prepared for transport. The original discovery at the site, the juvenile mammoth, is more spectacular with each day of excavation, with its pelvis and cervical vertebrae now exposed. Teams are also digging in the sloth pit, which is still producing various mastodon parts, and in a new peat site that has a disarticulated mammoth. As the logistical leader of the excavation, I end up doing a little of everything, which is fantastic. We have found something spectacular every single day. I should be used to it by now, but I'm still floored every time.

Some of the most exceptional specimens in this ancient lake are the plants. As a paleobotanist, I have a soft spot for a good fossil plant. Peel through a layer of the peat, and you'll find still green slender stems of

The Miller diggers: Dane, Liz, and Ian.

whole sedges. In fact, the peat itself is a fossil, made entirely of plant parts. As I sift through it, I find spruce and fir cones, iridescent beetles, and thousands of seeds.

Our first find on this day was a paleo-ecological kicker. Dan Fisher, one of the world's leading mastodon and mammoth scientists, handed me an arm-size branch he'd pulled from the peat. At first it looked like the many pieces of wood we'd already collected—dark colored, smooth, and wet. At second glance, my jaw dropped. One end of the branch had the telltale chew marks of a beaver. We'd just found evidence of our sixth mammal species at the site, and we'd done it with a piece of wood. Enthused as I was, however, nothing could prepare me for the find just moments away.

By late morning, I joined the blade runners. The bottom of the lake is particularly productive for isolated bones, and the dozers were getting close. I knew I had to keep a close eye. I heard the pop of freshly broken bone and saw a 3-foot chunk sticking out of the mud. It looked like another tusk, but it was a horn!

We immediately mobilized a team to dig the horn, slowly, steadily shaving the dirt away. Emerging to meet the sunny, warm late-fall day at 9,000 feet, after being buried tens of thousands of years, was the massive skull of an extinct ice age bison. Measuring more than 6 feet from horn tip to horn tip, this bison, an unprecedented find in the Rocky Mountains, dwarfs its modern cousin.

Skilled museum volunteers and staff spent the rest of the day exposing the skull and encasing it in plaster and burlap. At 5:30 p.m., it was fully plastered and ready to go. Mud-caked and soaked head to toe, we triumphantly head back to the condos, recounting stories of another great day of discovery.

By 9 p.m. dinner is done, and the bison is already on its way back to Denver. I'm tired and hope to hit the hay soon. Instead I sit down with my fellow scientists to discuss the day's finds. It's midnight before we know it. As we disperse to our rooms, someone comments, "Now this is what I got into the business for!" We can't wait to see what tomorrow holds.

This beaver-chewed stick was a big surprise.

The crew stops work to gawk as the amazing bison skull emerges from the ground.

map that Bryant attributed the formation of the Ziegler glacial lake to the Bull Lake glaciation, an event that occurred between 200,000 and 130,000 years ago, rather than to the more recent Pinedale glaciation, which peaked about 21,000 years ago. This geologic observation seemed to confirm Russ's suggestion that the bison spoke of a more ancient time.

Steve Holen, still hoping to find evidence of human hunters, was disappointed with the suggestion that the deposits in the lake might be too old for that. Then, Steve's wife, Kathy, surprised all of us by announcing the discovery of the molar from a baby mastodon that was probably less than

Baby mastodon tooth, shown at actual size.

three years old when it died along the shores of the lake. This was the first indication that the site held fossils of babies. Babies had died here, and that was food for thought. Any fossil site is like a crime scene, and clues to the nature of the Ziegler Reservoir crime were beginning to accumulate.

Museum educator Samantha Richards, who was visiting schools with the bones of the tent mammoth, was racking up amazing numbers. In five days of that first week, she visited more than 8,500 students in the Roaring Fork Valley, and we took to calling her Samammoth. This word play with Samantha's name made us start to fiddle around with the name Snowmass. What about Snowmammoth? Or Snowmastodon? That second one had a really nice ring to it, and we started thinking that Snowmass Village ought to change its name. I called my Alaskan artist friend Ray Troll to tell him about this idea. Ray is a musician who writes and records music about fossils, and I thought that he might rise to the occasion and make me a song. He loved the idea, and he and his music buddy Russell Wodehouse started working. I thought I could play the song at the upcoming Snowmass Village Town Council meeting as part of a farcical motion that the town change its name.

By November 7, the weather was cooling, and we were starting to get a better understanding of the anatomy of the ancient lake deposit. With the discovery of the bison, it had become clear that fossils actually were in the silt, but as we dug along the face of the future dam, we were finding out that the top of the moraine was quite complex.

More scientists arrived to help. Steve Jackson from the University of Wyoming, an expert on ice age plants, came with two of his graduate students, as did a trio of geologists from the U.S. Geological Survey in Denver. A week earlier, Ian had called the survey in search of help and spoke to Jeff Pigati, a radiocarbon expert; Tom Ager, a pollen and spore expert; and Paul Carrara, a glacial geologist. This was an interesting trio. Jeff is a young fresh spark of a guy who is relatively new at the USGS and relatively fresh from grad school. He brought a wealth of recent contacts with ice age specialists and up-to-date knowledge of the latest trends in

Bruce Bryant and his 1972 geologic map showing Ziegler Reservoir as a swampy depression surrounded by glacial moraine. The clues were there!

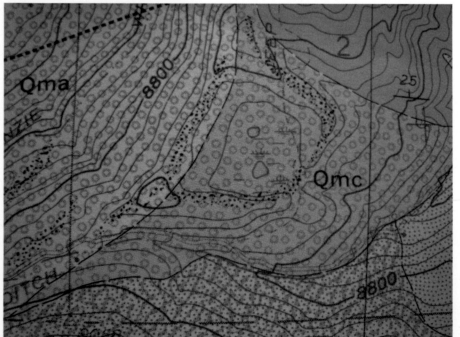

ice age science. Tom and Paul are senior scientists at the survey and they brought two careers of experience. Between the three of them, I was confident that we had both an awareness of new techniques and a deep well of experience to make sure that we could interpret the fossil site.

I was particularly pleased that Tom had joined our group. He studies fossil pollen and spore grains by taking thimble-sized samples of lake-bed clay and retrieving identifiable samples from the majority of the plants that lived alongside the lakeshore when that layer of mud accumulated on the lake floor. For me, this technique is like magic. A thimble of mud gives you a whole forest. Without a doubt, the pollen and spore story would be critical to our understanding of the site. We now had some firepower to direct at the mystery of the ancient lake, but in the meantime, the weather was beginning to deteriorate. We were in a race against winter.

By now some of the crew had been working for more than 10 days straight. The days began at six in the morning and ended around 10 at night, and signs of fatigue were beginning to show. We also had a steady stream of volunteers coming and going and were in a continuous mode of training new diggers.

My research assistant Carol noticed that we weren't doing such a good job in associating written data with all the bones that we were digging up.

I had been worrying about this as well, so I asked her to develop a numbering system for keeping track of all of the finds.

At one point, Dane Miller noticed that a big track hoe was digging in the clay that lay on top of the peat about 50 yards north of the tent. We had assumed that clay was barren of fossils because we had walked along with the dozers as they cleared a big stretch of clay on the far west side of the reservoir, without unearthing anything. Something possessed Dane to wander over and watch the track hoe. Just as he got there, the big bucket scooped through the side of a huge mammoth skull. Dane rushed over and saw a foot-long tooth and a portion of a tusk poking out of the sticky clay. He called off the track hoe, and Russ

Above: Carol Lucking, the team's data captain. *Left:* Samantha "Samammoth" Richards shares Snowmass bones with Roaring Fork students. *Right:* Help arrives from the U.S. Geological Survey. Jeff Pigati, Steve Holen, Tom Ager, and Paul Carrara (left to right) packing a lot of much-needed knowledge about the ice age.

Graham came over to inspect the find. It was a big fossil in very sticky clay, and there was no way that we would have time to fully excavate it. This fossil made us realize that we would have to come back in the spring. We called it the "Clay Mammoth," covered it with a tarp, and carefully buried it under a 2-foot pile of clay.

Gould was wrapping up for the year, and November 8 would be the last day that Jesse and the big D6 were down in the pit with us. We thought that we had worked out a good path for him to push dirt out of the hole. Ian and I ran the blade and Jesse took a couple of passes, pushing the dirt to the top of the hill. On the third pass, his blade exposed a big log. We got shovels and pried it out of the ground. It was about 4 feet long and at least 15 inches in diameter. We knew mastodons to be forest animals, but here was proof that they had lived in a forest at Ziegler Reservoir.

On the next pass, Jesse felt something with his blade. He lifted the blade and backed away to expose the 18-inch tip of a polished, perfectly beautiful big ivory mastodon tusk. I could see the tiniest mark where the blade had made contact with the tusk. The remainder of the tusk projected down into the ground. It would take hours to fully expose the tusk and get a plaster jacket on it—and it lay right in the middle of the bulldozer's push road. We agreed that this would be the last fossil to be found by the dozer and released Jesse to excavate clay on the far western side of the site where Gould was beginning to stockpile material to build the dam.

The next day, with snow falling pretty heavily, we figured that we had less than a week before we would have to give up for the winter. As we worked to expose the big tusk, we were surprised to see that it was jumbled up with big angular boulders that weighed up to a hundred pounds, masses of twigs, and branches. What kind of an environment would bury complete tusks with rocks and logs? As we trenched around the tusk to make room to apply the plaster jacket, water seeped out of the ground and filled the trench, threatening to overtop our rubber boots. I started digging a trench to drain the water from the tusk trench. As I dug, I found more rocks and branches. And I started finding bone as well. Soon I got other diggers working to extend my trench, and they also started to find bones.

Frank Sanders removes the sediment from the broken tip of the big mastodon tusk.

Dave Gyolai, another Gould equipment operator, brought over a small track hoe with rubber tracks, called a mini-excavator, to help us move the muck that we had already shoveled and pull some of the large boulders out of the ground. Like Jesse, he could feel the ground through the vibration of his machine. After one deep scoop, he pulled up short and said, "I think I just hit a bone." As he lifted the bucket out of the hole, a surging stream of clear water flowed out of the side of the hole. Dane and Ian crawled into the hole and started digging with hand tools; within minutes, a nearly perfect mastodon tibia lay at the bottom of the hole. Dane gingerly picked it up and held it above his head. Clear water continued to pour out of the bone like it was a fossil kitchen sponge. I looked at Ian, he looked at me, and I twisted my neck down and took a big swallow. Who needs Perrier when you can drink mastodon juice? We passed the bone around, and the brave and foolish amongst us followed my lead.

Dave is a big, gruff, bearded guy who seemed hard to make laugh. When Dane passed him the bone, Dave cradled it in his arms like he was holding a baby. A sly smile crept across his face, and we had our first Flintstone moment.

I've been on lots of fossil sites, but I had never been to one where the bones were so well

preserved that you could pick them up and fondle them without worrying that they would crack or fall apart in your hands. Here at Snowmass, we could hold the bone high and savor the moment of discovery. It was a sublime experience.

On November 10, I spoke at a Snowmass Rotary meeting and showed images that I had taken the day before. The Rotarians were clearly thrilled to be seeing a first-hand account of the unfolding discovery. After breakfast, I rushed back to the site, eager to be digging. The water in the trenches had frozen overnight, and the first few inches of dirt in the shoveled piles were frozen into a rigid crust. We only had a few days left.

Ian made a critical observation. He realized that the layer of rocks, bones, logs, and clay had a bottom and that it was underlain by a layer of dark gray silt. The silt was soft and smooth and easy to dig while the bouldery

Above left: Dave Gyolai with a mastodon tibia, which would become known as the Magic Tibia, and the team's first Flintstone moment. *Above right:* Dane Miller unearths the tibia. *Left:* The mini-excavator helps to pull away dirt, and we clear the area around the big tusk.

bony layer was compact and difficult to break. He realized two things: The first was that digging directly into the bony layer was not only difficult, but you stood a good chance of damaging the bones with your shovel. The second was that if you dug into the silt below, you could undercut the bony layer and it would collapse in a way that would expose the bones without harming them. Soon we were all digging smart by undercutting the bank and exposing bone after bone. It also became quite apparent that the bone zone was a distinct layer about 2 feet thick that could best be described as a buried debris flow. However these animals had come to die at Ziegler; it was a submarine landslide that had finally entombed their scattered bones on the lake floor. Things were beginning to make sense, and we also had a good method for mining bones.

I consulted with Russ Graham and we devised a method to measure the location of each bone. We pounded a length of steel rebar into the ground and tied a rope to it. Whenever we found a bone, we would stretch to rope to the bone and measure the distance and orientation to the rebar. We also measured the orientation and tilt of the bone itself. Our goal was to collect enough data so that we could rebuild the deposit digitally, using the resulting information to solve the mystery of how the animals had died. We gave a field number to the rebar and a sample number to each bone before we labeled and bagged it. In this way we could dig fast and still capture the data we needed.

It was insanely fun, collapsing the debris flow and plucking bones. For a while, I was digging by myself and finding a new bone every six or seven minutes. It felt like we had cracked part of the code of the site.

That night we finally took a night off and went to the Mountain Dragon for several well-deserved beers. We had forged into a tight team on a curious mission in a race against the weather. We were our own reality television show. While we were digging, Ian's mom and her helpers were shopping, cooking, getting supplies, and checking people in and out of the condos. Down at the Water and Sanitation offices, Carol Lucking worked with a team of conservators from the museum who were washing, labeling, and packing the bones. Our public relations team was setting up media interviews and guiding reporters to the site. The museum's digital media team was producing daily video updates for the web. National Geographic sent a variety of still and video camera people to the site. It really does take a village to dig a hole.

Each night at six o'clock, I would call in to the museum and conference with key folks to make sure that we were coordinating the other aspects of the dig. For all the work we were doing in Snowmass, dozens of people back in Denver were being kept busy by the dig as well. Video that we shot during the day was edited and shipped to Denver, where it was posted on our website the next morning so people could follow the dig day by day. It was real time paleontology with up-to-the-moment reporting.

Mammoth and Mastodon Madness
THURSDAY, NOVEMBER 11—MONDAY, NOVEMBER 15, 2010

The Snowmass Village Town Council visited the site on November 11 and they began to take stock of what was rapidly turning into a major opportunity for the town. Kit started allowing tours to visit the site. Kit's daughters, Ashley and Jenny, had played a major role interpreting the bones when they were on display at the Water and San office, and they now appeared in the role of tour guides, leading busload after busload of interested locals to the site. We were increasingly nervous about the tours.

A layer of smooth, dark gray silt is overlain by the debris flow that includes rocks, branches, and bones in a matrix of clay, silt, and sand. The hammer rests on a bone.

Not only did the visitors distract us from the digging, but slippery clay in an active construction site presented a real hazard, and I was really worried that someone would fall and get hurt. Fortunately, Ashley and Jenny did a great job of outfitting the visitors in hard hats and security vests and helping 90-year-olds and 4-year-olds, alike, pick their way through the muddy site.

On November 11, we received the much-anticipated radiocarbon dates, and the results were stunning. Both analyses suggested that the site was more than 45,000 years old. Russ Graham had been right with his hunch about the big bison. Steve Holen was disappointed. For him the site was considerably less interesting if there was no possibility that human hunters had been involved. Rather than being an archaeological site (one that involved humans), the analyses seemed to confirm that this was a paleontological site (no humans). Since paleontologists and archaeologists use different techniques, this would change how we moved forward with the dig. I was thrilled. It now looked like we were dealing with an extraordinarily well-preserved, very ancient site.

In the tent, our team carefully photographed the exposed skeleton of the young mammoth and then carefully mapped and collected each bone. The tent, which had propane heat, was where we stored our food and gear. As the weather grew worse, the tent became an odd steamy sanctuary in a dark and snowy mud field. As the team neared completion of the mammoth excavation, they moved to the bison that we had found in the peat. They set up a small tent and worked rapidly to map and remove those bones. At least a few of the bison's leg bones appeared to be oriented down into the peat, raising the interesting possibility that the animal had gotten bogged down in the ancient mire. That idea grew into our default scenario for how the animals in the peat were trapped and eventually buried.

With growing interest in the site, we had decided to hold an open house in the Snowmass Base Village on November 13. A team of 14 educators from the museum drove up on the evening of the 12th to set up for the event. By this time we had a pretty good sense of the main questions people were likely to ask. We also knew that people of different ages and differing levels of interest could be reached in different ways. Finally, we

Left: As the excavation progressed, more of Jesse's mammoth became visible. *Right:* A young female mammoth gets stuck in the mud and it looks like it might be fatal.

Top: People crowd the conference center for the open house. *Middle:* Covered in fresh mud, Kirk answers questions about the site. *Bottom:* Kids get to practice their digging skills.

knew that people of all ages were really interested in the site and wanted to see the actual bones that we were finding. Still, we had no idea of just how many people would actually show up on a snowy day in peak mud season. I started the morning by taking the educator team to the site and showing them the mammoth in the tent, the bison in the peat, and our diggings in the debris flow deposits down in the hole. They were thrilled to visit the site, and it amped their already high commitment to quality education.

While I was chatting with our educators, I looked across the pit and spotted Frank Sanders, one of our more versatile volunteers, walking down the slippery clay slope into the pit. I saw him slip and sit down. He didn't get up. I thought that he was just gathering his wits, and didn't think anything of it. Ten minutes later, when the tour ended, I realized that he was still sitting there. I went over to him and realized that he had fallen and could not get up. Frank's ankle, after several hours of surgery and a lot of stainless steel screws and plates, was our first casualty.

At 10 a.m., when the Mammoth and Mastodon Madness event in the Base Village ballroom opened its doors, a long line of eager visitors was already waiting. People filed in and were greeted by wall-sized images of ice age mammoths, mastodons, sloths, and bison; tables weighted with freshly dug tusks and bones; and interactive games tailored for kids of different ages. Each hour, on the hour, either Ian or I would drive down from the dig and stand in front of the crowd, covered with mud, and answer questions. As the day went on, more people arrived and the lines grew longer. The wait time climbed, exceeding two hours. The event was an amazing success. In a town with 2,800 full-time residents, more than 3,700 people came to our event. Watching this event unfold, I began to realize that was not just a dig—it was a movement.

As I was leaving from one of my hourly updates, a formidable woman in the line yelled out my name. I thought that she wanted to complain about the long wait, but it was just the opposite. The woman was Georgia Hanson, head of the Aspen Historical Society. Amazingly, Georgia had been at the lunch in Rapid City back in September when I had spoken about the importance of fossil discoveries to small towns. Even before the discovery of October 14, she had tried to contact me to get me to come speak about fossils in the Roaring Fork Valley. Her plan was rapidly turning into reality.

I went back and forth from the dig site to the Base Village four times that day, each time bringing new stories of fossil discovery to an ever-changing and fully engaged audience. It was so fun to be sharing the dig, as it was happening, with thousands of people. On the drive back up the hill, I started thinking about Amory Lovins, the brilliant founder of the Rocky Mountain Institute. I had been reading his work and watching him lecture for years. I don't like to use the word "genius," but Lovins's talks always leave me feeling that he is visiting us from the future. I had briefly met him at a fund-raiser the previous year, and we had traded business cards. I had his card in my wallet and recalled he was a resident of Old Snowmass, just down the valley a few miles. I thought it would be interesting to take a futurist to the distant past, so I called him. He answered the phone on the third ring and was initially puzzled

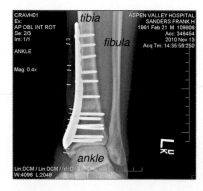

An X-ray of Frank Sanders' leg after it was repaired by Aspen surgeons.

The Ziegler Reservoir excavation at 2 p.m. on November 15, 2010. Gould Construction's porta-potty and dump trucks remain, as does the Snowmass Water and Sanitation District's tent, which covers the mammoth discovery site. Winter has halted construction on the reservoir, and the DMNS crew has given up its fight against winter and retreated from the site.

about who I was and why I was calling. Eventually I convinced him that he shouldn't miss history, especially when it was happening in his neighborhood. Later that afternoon, on what turned out to be 63rd birthday, he and his wife, Judith, drove to the site, and I had the pleasure of watching that crazy smart engineering brain of his apply itself to the puzzle of the Snowmass dig. Lovins left me with a host of ideas about scanning, digitizing, and hydraulically mining the bones. The hole was turning into a hero lure.

The next day, the team completed removing all the remains of the mammoth from the tent and turned their concentration to finishing the bison on the peat. My artist friend Jan Vriesen from Milaca, Minnesota, arrived around midday. I had invited him to Snowmass to paint a series of paintings of the site through its evolution. Jan and I have been collaborating since 1993, when we worked together to build two dioramas for the museum's *Prehistoric Journey* exhibit. Jan is one of those miraculous painters who can effortlessly create gorgeous landscapes. Over the years, he and I had learned that we teamed up well to reconstruct extinct landscapes, lost worlds from deep time. As the paleontologist, I would supply the concept and the fossils. Jan would compose and paint the image. The results were compelling and plausible views of these lost worlds. Over the last 15 years, we had worked together on nearly two dozen different ancient landscape projects. I knew that I needed him in Snowmass.

Besides being a skilled and quick painter, Jan is an utterly delightful person who charms everyone in his immediate proximity. On a tour around the site we scoped out the concept for five different paintings: the site shortly after the basin was formed by a glacier, roughly 130,000 years ago; the site when it was inhabited by mastodons, sloths, and giant bison about 120,000 years ago; the site when it was inhabited by mammoths, bison, and deer about 70,000 years ago; the site as it looked on November 15, 2010, and the site as it would look in June 2012 after the reservoir had been completed. We picked a spot high on the slope of the moraine on the north side of the lake that would be the perspective for all five paintings. Jan nestled down between a pair of sagebrush and spent the rest of the afternoon in that spot, watching the clouds pass and the light change. By the time he left the next morning, he was ready to begin painting.

Retreat to Denver
MONDAY, NOVEMBER 15–TUESDAY, NOVEMBER 16, 2010

On November 15, with heavy, wet snow falling, we conceded defeat to the elements and the dig ended. The diggers would cede Snowmass back to the skiers. Ian led the effort to clear our gear off the hill. The team tarped and buried the excavation sites for the mammoth and the bison with the thought that we would come back in the spring and finish the job.

Ian and I went to the Water and San offices to meet with Kit, Joe Enzer, and the engineers from URS to try to figure out what we needed to do next. It was clear to everyone that this amazing high-elevation ice age site was just beginning to yield its secrets and that Ziegler Reservoir would have to accommodate some serious paleontology before its construction project could be completed.

I knew that this was not only the best find of my career but also the best find of the museum's 110-year history, and I was committed to make it work. Fortunately, Kit also saw the bigger picture, and we agreed to work together to make both the fossil dig and dam construction a success in 2011.

During this meeting, I learned an interesting fact from John Sikora, the lead engineer on the reservoir project. The presence of the lake-bed silt was a structural factor in the construction of the dam. If the silt was overloaded or if the area was shaken by a significant earthquake, it was possible there could be dangerous compaction or liquefaction. This had the potential to compromise the structural integrity of the dam, a serious matter since the dam was above the village. For this reason, John wanted to make sure that all of the silt was removed from the footing of the dam before dam construction began. I quipped that an earthquake didn't seem likely, but John informed me that the West Elk Mountains were some of the most seismically active places in Colorado. This information would come in handy in the very near future.

I had one last thing to do that Monday. I needed to make an appearance at the Snowmass Village Town Council meeting and make sure the fossil site was accurately represented to the town's elected officials. I also had an ulterior motive. Ray and Russell had completed the first version of their Snowmastodon song. I had heard that Councilman Reed Lewis was a big fan of the band Widespread Panic and that he was going to propose their song, "Big Wooly Mammoth," to be the official song of Snowmass Village. Now it's not that I don't like Widespread Panic; it's just that Snowmass's mammoth was a Columbian mammoth and that Ray had a new song called "Snowmastodon" that was tailor made for the town.

I had asked Ray to e-mail me the song, which he did as I was driving to the city building. Unfortunately, I was new to my iPhone and didn't know how to get the song to play from the e-mail. I watched helplessly as the Town Council voted in "Big Wooly Mammoth" as their official song.

The rest of the meeting went very well, with the mayor and the council expressing tremendous support for the dig and recognizing its importance for the town. By the end of the meeting they agreed to appoint an Ice Age Discovery Committee to explore how the town might best benefit from the dig. Mayor Boineau thanked me for the museum's hard work and urged us to return in the spring.

The next day, I loaded two tusks coated in plaster in the back of Big Blue, the museum's fossil-hauling truck, and headed for I-70. I was driving alone, and Vail Pass was an icy mess. Coming down from the Eisenhower Tunnel, the highway was covered with black ice, and I saw several cars in the ditch. I drove slowly and they closed the highway behind me. Ian and the rest of the team had to take a detour over Hoosier Pass and didn't get into Denver until late that night. Carol Lucking and her helpers were smarter, waiting out the storm in the Glenwood Hot Springs.

SNOWMASTODON (YEAH, YEAH!)

©2010 Troll/Wodehouse   Music by: Russell Wodehouse   Lyrics by: Ray Troll & Russell Wodehouse

Jesse Steele was driving a bulldozer, so many things that man went rolling over
When one day springing up from the ground, something strange and amazing he found
The very last thing Jesse had been counting on was running over an ancient ice age mastodon
Working hard to expand the Ziegler Reservoir. It started lookin' like a prehistoric abattoir
Snowmastodon—so big and hairy. Snowmastodon—so freakin' scary
Who can tell me why, why have you come and gone?
My hands are black my lips are blue now here's to you … Snowmastodon!

Dr. J and the crew from DMNS, grabbed their shovels and Big Blue and they headed west
Running blade paid in spades; I heard Ian shout, "It's Miller time, I got mine, hey man check it out!"
A mile high in the sky in the mountain peat, *Megalonyx*, mammoths, and some other beasts
Thirty thousand years since the light of day, c'mon, c'mon! Let me, let me hear you say!

Yeah, yeah! Let's party on! Yeah, yeah! We got it going on. Yeah, yeah! I love Donkey Kong.

Not long ago in the days of the Pleistocene this land of ours was an elephant's dream—yeah
From sea to sea, buried deep in the clay and sand, mega beasts of the ice age ruled the land!
Digging in the dirt from dawn to dusk, Mountain Dragon gang waiting on the tusks
Deer and beaver, beetles and the *latifrons*, can you dig it now? We got it going on!

Yeah, yeah! Let's party on! Yeah, yeah! We got it going on. Yeah, yeah! I love Donkey Kong.

When I pulled into the museum's loading dock around 5 p.m., I was greeted by a dozen excited staff who were waiting with a forklift to unload the 400-pound plaster jackets. I was so tired that I couldn't even make conversation. I just wandered around and mumbled as they unloaded the tusks. I haven't been that tired since I worked a 24-hour shift at a salmon cannery back in the 1970s.

Round one of the Snowmass dig was over, and the Denver Museum of Nature & Science was suddenly in the ice age business. In 19 calendar days (October 29 to November 16), a total of 67 museum staff and trained volunteers had logged 3,634 hours of work (454 person days) and had collected more than 600 bones. This epic effort was just a taste of what was to come.

The site itself was truly significant. It was at a high elevation, contained superbly preserved plant and animal fossils from multiple hori-

zons, and appeared to span a lot of interesting and important geologic time. All in all, it was a bona fide big discovery, one for the history books. At least that was its potential. Whether we could achieve that potential would say a lot more about us than it would about the site. We had done a great job of digging with little notice. But could we bring it home and deliver on the scientific potential of the site? That was the question that was rattling around in my head the next morning.

Left: Moving a plaster-coated mastodon tusk into the bed of Big Blue. *Right:* Moving a plaster-jacketed mastodon tusk from the museum's loading dock to the collection storage room. *Opposite:* Snow-capped Mount Daly towers over Ziegler Reservoir, making it one of the prettiest fossil sites in the world. *Next page:* Aerial photograph of Snowmass Village and Snowmass ski area looking south. Ziegler Reservoir is the round, flat spot in the lower right corner.

ACT TWO

Drying Bones and Sorting Scientists

WEDNESDAY, NOVEMBER 17—THURSDAY, NOVEMBER 25, 2010

In a way, the arrival of winter was the best thing that could have happened to us. The discovery had been made, and we had sprinted for 19 days to salvage the bones that were being exposed, but winter made sure that we all stopped and thought about how to do the spring dig better. Kit had planned his reservoir project so that he would do the excavation in 2010 and the construction in 2011. They had completed nearly all of their excavation before they hit bones, so we didn't mess up their schedule. That gave me six whole months to carefully plan my next steps. Sprint, pause and think, then execute. I couldn't have asked for a better schedule.

The first thing I needed to do was to make sure that we hadn't exaggerated the significance of the find. I had been careful and had consulted the best scientists I knew, but I was about to commit the museum to an even larger effort in the spring and I wanted to make sure my ducks were in a row. The best way to do that was to get a lot of smart people talking. We had already hosted a number of great scientists on the site, and I figured that they would form the core science team. I would use them to help me form a plan and select a broader team so that we covered the diversity of scientific opportunities that were represented by the site.

On November 17, I formalized the core team of 11 scientists and scheduled a conference call to begin the planning for the spring. On that call, we decided that we needed to add an expert on ancient-DNA to the core team.

In early 2009, I had attended a conference in Merida, Mexico, where I was blown away by the science and communication skills of an ancient DNA scientist from Penn State named Beth Shapiro. Later, I researched her background and discovered that not only was she widely published in the study of ancient DNA, but that she was also a Rhodes Scholar, a MacArthur "Genius Grant" recipient, and a National Geographic Explorer-in-Residence. Any one of those awards would be a career capper, and she wasn't even 40 yet. Russ Graham called her up, and we had the 12th and final member of the core team.

Then, we set about assembling a more comprehensive science team, one that could fully cover the range of geology and fossils that the site had and would potentially yield. Over a series of conference calls, we defined a number of key characteristics that members of the team would share. They had to be top-notch scientists who could bring a unique skill set or knowledge base to the group; they had to have good reputations for working in groups and publishing their work rapidly; they had to be willing to donate their time to the project; they had to be willing to help us raise funds to make the project work; and they had to be available in May and June.

Meanwhile, back at the museum, I was also organizing the groups that would fill out the rest of the project. The science team was central to the long-term significance of the project, but to get the work done we also had to have our act together with the logistics of the excavation; the preservation, conservation, preparation, and curation of the fossils; the coordination of the media; fund-raising; grant writing; accounting; legal issues; and educational outreach. In addition, we were negotiating with National Geographic Television to do an hour-long documentary, and we were talking with the Town of Snowmass Village about building a small visitors' center about the dig on the Snowmass mall. This project was shaping up to be a perfect fit with our mission: The Denver Museum of Nature & Science inspires curiosity and excites minds of all ages through scientific discovery and the presentation and preservation of the world's unique treasures.

Our exhibits department is run by an incredibly competent, detail-oriented woman named Jodi Schoemer. Back in October, she was assigned the task of managing the exhibits, outreach, and documentation side of this rapidly growing project. While I was in Snowmass, she ran the operation back in Denver, coordinating all of the activities the museum was doing to support our efforts in the field. I am truly amazed at how Jodi solves problems. Basically, she breaks a situation down into hundreds of component parts and then sorts out contingencies for each part. Where I would see 10 elements to a problem, she would see 73. She is a great person to have your back, and I was psyched that she had ours.

One of the first things we did when we got back to Denver was to host a press conference. We had created so much excitement in the Roaring Fork Valley that we wanted to share it with our primary audience. We held the event on November 18 in the museum's gorgeous Leprino Family Atrium. The view to the west from this spot is the best view in Denver, and on that day, the snowy Rockies were direct evidence of the weather that was busily burying our recently evacuated excavation back in Snowmass.

George Sparks opened the event, speaking about how this was a singular moment in history, a very significant discovery for the museum, and a life-changing event for those of us who were involved. George is a genuine

individual, and when he speaks from the heart, he packs a pretty powerful emotional punch. Listening to him speak, it really struck me that history was being made. Over the previous year, I had been working with my staff to write a history of the Denver Museum of Nature & Science. It was pretty clear that the museum's most significant discovery to date was the 1927 find of projectile points in association with ice age bison near the town of Folsom, New Mexico. This was the first discovery to firmly establish the presence of humans in North America during the very end of the ice age. I wondered if Snowmass would be more important than Folsom.

It was also great to see so many museum staff and volunteers. The Denver-based team had done so much to support us when we were in Snowmass, so it was great to share the excitement of the discovery with them. In his comments, Steve Holen pointed out that only three partial mastodons had ever been found in Colorado and that a Jefferson's ground sloth had never before been found at elevations this high anywhere in North America.

The next day, Jodi and I sat down and agreed that the project needed a name. For a while we had toyed with calling it the Snowmass Mammoth Project, but I really liked the ring of "Snowmastodon." The two of us agreed that the formal, trademarked name would be the Snowmastodon Project.

On November 20, the museum hosted Denver's version of the Mammoth and Mastodon Madness day that had rocked Snowmass a week before. We were curious to see if Denverites loved mammoths as much as the Snowmass Villagers. They did. Nearly 5,000 people showed up at the museum to see the bones from Snowmass. We also brought out some ice age mammal skeletons from our collection storage vaults. Many years ago the museum had traded some fossils with the Los Angeles County Museum, and in return we received an amazing collection of skeletons from the famous La Brea Tar Pits. Our collection included two saber-toothed cats, two dire wolves, a bison, a horse, and a Harlan's ground sloth.

The sloth is a great big grizzly-bear-sized skeleton mounted on a wheeled platform. Our curmudgeonly collection manager hates to move the beast, but he relented and the crowds were able to get a great show-

An emotional Steve Holen, mastodon tusk
at hand, speaks at the press conference in
Denver on November 18.

THE SNOWMASTODON SCIENCE TEAM

By early November, Ian Miller, Richard Stucky, Steve Holen, and I realized that the Snowmass discovery was much larger than we could handle with the scientific staff at the Denver Museum of Nature & Science (DMNS). We recruited additional scientists to expand the expertise of the group, bringing the intellectual firepower to deliver world-class science. Ian contacted Jeff Pigati at the U.S. Geological Survey (USGS) in Denver, and Jeff led us to a trove of ice age experts. In all, we built a team of 37 scientists from 19 institutions and four countries. We organized this team into five groups based on different scientific disciplines.

THE BONE PEOPLE

Zoologists, biochemists, vertebrate paleontologists, and archaeologists are the scientists responsible for understanding vertebrate animals and their DNA.

John Demboski
DMNS
ground squirrels

Dan Fisher
Univ. of Michigan
fossil elephants

Russ Graham
Pennsylvania State Univ.
ice age mammals

Kirk Hansen
Univ. of Colorado at Denver
fossil protein

Steve Holen
DMNS
ancient humans

Greg McDonald
National Park Service
sloth fossils

Cody Newton
Univ. of Colorado
bison fossils

Hendrik Poinar
McMaster Univ.
mammoth DNA

Adam Rountrey
Univ. of Michigan
fossil elephants

Joe Sertich
DMNS
dinosaur fossils

Beth Shapiro
Pennsylvania State Univ.
ancient DNA

Mathias Stiller
Pennsylvania State Univ.
ancient DNA

Richard Stucky
DMNS
mammal fossils

THE ROCK PEOPLE

Geologists, geochemists, and stratigraphers are the scientists responsible for understanding the lake-filling sediments and the sequence of sediment layers.

Bruce Bryant
USGS
geologic mapping

Paul Carrara
USGS
glacial geology

Jeff Honke
USGS
sediment coring

Kirk Johnson
DMNS
stratigraphy

Dan Muhs
USGS
windblown sediment

Joe Street
Stanford Univ.
geochemistry

THE PLANT PEOPLE

Paleobotanists, palynologists, and dendrochronologists are the scientists responsible for understanding the various types of fossil plants found in the lake bed sediment.

Scott Anderson
Northern
Arizona Univ.
fossil pollen

Tom Ager
USGS
fossil pollen

Dick Baker
Univ. of Iowa
fossil seeds

Steve Jackson
Univ. of Wyoming
fossil plants

Gonzalo Jimenez-
Moreno
Univ. of Granada
fossil pollen

Ian Miller
DMNS
fossil plants

Steve Nash
DMNS
tree rings

Laura Strickland
USGS
fossil seeds

THE TIME PEOPLE

Geochronologists are the scientists who use various techniques to measure the age of fossils, rocks, and sediments.

Nat Lifton
Purdue Univ.
cosmogenic dating

Shannon Mahan
USGS
OSL dating

Jim Paces
USGS
U-series dating

Jeff Pigati
USGS
*radiocarbon
dating*

THE BUG PEOPLE

Paleoentomologists and invertebrate paleontologists are the scientists who study fossil insects and freshwater invertebrates.

Jordan Bright
Univ. of Arizona
fairy shrimp

Les Cwynar,
Univ. of New
Brunswick
midge fossils

Scott Elias
Royal Holloway Univ.
fossil bugs

Dave Porinchu
Ohio State Univ.
midge fossils

Saxon Sharpe
Desert Research
Institute
fossil snails

Sarah Spaulding
USGS
*freshwater
plankton*

ing of the incredible skeleton. People are always amazed when a paleontologist picks up a fossil bone and knows what kind of animal it comes from. "Oh yeah, that's a bison femur." What really makes this possible is that fossil bone specialists have trained in museums where entire skeletons are stored in what are called comparative collections, giving the specialists lots of practice looking at various kinds of fossil skeletons.

We also had face painters who applied tusks to our visitors, touchable bones, places for kids to dig, and a host of educators who happily took people back in time to the Colorado ice age. My dad and sister were visiting for Thanksgiving, and it was pretty fun to see them tusk-faced and delighted by our ice age spectacular.

By this time, I had been doing nothing but Snowmass for a solid month, and my regular workload was starting to back up. Of course, being the chief curator of a natural history museum, my workload doesn't always look like work. On November 26, I laid down my Snowmass tasks and departed Denver with two dozen board members for the Brazilian Amazon.

Left: Mammoth and Mastodon Madness strikes the Denver Museum of Nature & Science. *Below:* Kirk's sister, Kirsten, all tusked up. *Right:* This skeleton of Harlan's ground sloth was excavated at the La Brea site in downtown Los Angeles. *Opposite:* The Amazon River is an amazing interaction of water and forest, with annual floods exceeding 30 feet.

Side Trip to Sloth City
FRIDAY, NOVEMBER 26—MONDAY, DECEMBER 6, 2010

For my whole life, "Amazon" was one of those simple words (like "Patagonia," "Gobi," or "Sahara") that conjured thoughts of mystery and exploration. As an avid reader of *National Geographic,* I devoured stories of expeditions to the jungles of South America. In 1994 a college friend called to tell me that she had just been to Brazil and had met a guy that I simply had to meet. He was an Amazonian *caboclo* (a river person of mixed European and Indian descent) named Moacir Fortes Pereira, who lived in the city of Manaus in the Brazilian state of Amazonas at the confluence of the Solimoes River (the main body of the Amazon) and its largest tributary, the Rio Negro. Moacir, or Mo, as he liked to be called, owned a river boat that he hired out to scientists or tourists who really wanted to see the

backwaters of the world's largest river. I called Mo, and he talked me into renting his boat and guide services for a two-week river trip. I then talked a dozen close friends into joining me, and later that year, we had the time of our lives exploring the river and the huge rain forest that flanks it.

On that first trip, I caught a terrible tropical disease. The main symptom of this disease was that I needed to return to the Amazon on a regular basis, and over the next 16 years, I would visit Mo a dozen times. Each time I would take a boatload of friends, artists, and scientists from North and South America.

One of the things that happens when you mix artists and scientists is that you often end up creating books and museum exhibits. One of my earlier Amazon trips triggered Miami Science Museum exhibit developer Sean Duran to collaborate with artist Ray Troll to create a traveling museum exhibit called *Amazon Voyage, Vicious Fishes and other Riches*. They had first opened the show in Miami in 2006, and in 2010, it finally came

to Denver. The show opened in late September, a few weeks before the Snowmass discovery. Mo and his son Mo Junior had come to Denver, and on October 12, I took them on an eight-hour flight in a small plane from Boulder, Colorado, to Page, Arizona, and back, to show them the wonders of the Colorado Plateau and the Colorado Rockies—my small repayment for showing me the wonders of Amazonia. On this gorgeous fall day we had clear, calm air as we crossed the Continental Divide and headed for Moab, Utah. We passed right over the Roaring Fork Valley, and I remember being awed by the fall colors on the slopes of Mount Sopris. We didn't happen to notice the Ziegler Reservoir excavation, which was well under way below our left wing. Little did I know that Jesse would find his mammoth just two days later.

The Colorado Plateau is arguably the best place in the world to see exposed layers of sedimentary rock. The Colorado River and its tributaries have sawed their way down into the earth, creating endless outcrops, can-

yons, badlands, mesas, and buttes. For a fossil guy like me, the Colorado Plateau is like an open book of our planet's history. For my two Amazonians, it was more rock that they could even imagine.

After the Colorado Plateau flight, Mo and his son returned to Brazil, Jesse found the mammoth, we spent 19 days digging, and then I headed to Brazil with the museum's trustees. This trip was different from earlier ones because now I knew that the Rocky Mountains had once been home to giant sloths. This fact greatly increased my interest in Amazonian sloths and their connection to Colorado.

On November 26, Mo and Mo Junior greeted us at the airport in Manaus, and we boarded Mo's boat and headed up the Rio Negro into the world's largest tropical rain forest. It was an amazing transition to go from digging ivory mastodon tusks in the snow at 8,875 feet to snorkeling in a river at the equator—and what a great way to recover. Why is this digression at all relevant to this book? The answer is sloths. The upper Amazon is chockablock with three-toed sloths.

Mo would take us out in small boats in the middle of the night to

Left: Board members from the Denver Museum of Nature & Science visit a very large tree on the Rio Negro. Moacir Fortes is on the far right. *Right:* Few things are more sublime than the smile of a three-toed tree sloth.

spotlight for wildlife. We would see all sorts of animals, from caiman (alligators) to boa constrictors and tree porcupines to iguanas, but the most common mammal we saw was the three-toed sloth.

Talk about an absurd animal. Three-toed sloths weigh not much more than 10 pounds, are maybe 30 inches tall, and hang out, motionless, high up on the branches of trees. They eat leaves and lead lives of stultifying boredom. They avoid being eaten by snakes, harpy eagles, and jaguars by being incredibly still. When they do move, they move in super slow motion. They have big claws on their hands and feet that rest in the closed position. This allows them to hang from a branch by their claws and fall asleep without falling off.

Mo's crew is composed of lithe, muscled caboclos who can climb trees with ease. When we spotted a sloth high up in a tree, Mo routinely dispatched one of his guys to climb up and get it. Improbable as it seems, these guys would scramble out of the boats and climb 50 or 60 feet up a tree and out onto a thin branch, often with a machete in their teeth. The sloth would see them coming and try to escape, very slowly. Inevitably, the caboclo would overtake the sloth and grab it by the scruff of its neck. Now the caboclo had to climb down a tree while holding a machete and a sloth. At night. I know that this sounds impossible, but I have watched it dozens of times. And that is how it has come to be that I have held and closely inspected dozens of three-toed sloths.

Glyptodonts, like these skeletons at a museum in La Plata, Argentina, are extinct relatives of sloths, armadillos, and anteaters. Like giant sloths, glyptodonts sauntered across the Isthmus of Panama into North America.

Sloths are members of an order of mammals known as the xenarthrans. This bizarre group first evolved in South America around 60 million years ago, and it was in South America that the giant sloths first appeared. Since all giant ground sloths are now extinct, their story is told only by fossils. Their cute, slow, arboreal relatives, the tree sloths, provide only the slightest hints about the nature and evolution of giant slothdom.

On close inspection, these small, slow, leaf-eating tree sloths show many of the same features of the giant ground sloths. Both have clawed hands and feet; both are vegetarians that eat leaves and other low-quality produce; and both just look odd.

The South America fossil record is awash in giant ground sloths and their bizarre relatives, the armadillo-like but Volkswagen-sized glyptodonts. There are more than 60 species of giant extinct South American ground sloths, some of which were as large as elephants. Sometime around 6 million years ago, the island continent of South America moved close enough to the peninsula of Central America so that giant ground sloths, which were excellent long-distance swimmers, were able to swim from South America to North America. Three million years ago, the continents had connected, forming the Isthmus of Panama, and sloths could walk where they once swam.

Four genera of giant ground sloths made the trek, and by the ice age, North America had a sloth problem. The largest of the four, a 5-ton elephant-sized monster known as *Eremotherium,* hugged the Gulf Coast, and its fossils are found from Texas to Daytona Beach, Florida. *Megalonyx* had the run of the continent and ended up as fossils in places as widely flung as Kentucky, Iowa, and Alaska.

In February 1961, excavations for a light tower on a runway at the Seattle-Tacoma International Airport uncovered a *Megalonyx* skeleton that was nearly complete except for its skull. When I was 12, I started haunting the back rooms of the Burke Museum in Seattle, where I pestered patient paleontologists. They tolerated my persistence and rewarded me with insiders' tales of local fossils. Stories of the headless sloth from the airport were woven into the fabric of my teenaged, fossil-obsessed brain.

One thing I knew for sure about the upcoming dig was that I wanted to find the skull of *Megalonyx.*

Queue the Salamanders
TUESDAY, DECEMBER 7–FRIDAY, DECEMBER 31, 2010

Apparently even a trip to the Amazon could not clear my mind of thoughts of Snowmass. The trip only lasted eight days, and then I was back on task. While I was away, the pickers of small fossils had been at work and a whole new Snowmass world was starting to come into view. It is curious that fossils, and the scientists who study them, are often categorized by size. You hear of microfossils, mesofossils, macrofossils, and megafossils. All of these names reflect the fact that similar-sized parts of organisms end up being fossilized together. Microfossils usually require a microscope to be seen, while mesofossils can be observed through a hand lens; macrofossils can be held in your hand, and megafossils may require a winch. Then there are the micropaleontologists and the macro folks. And of course fossils come from different organisms to start with: mammals, clams, insects, trees, shrubs, herbs, amphibians, fungi, and algae. One of the benefits of having a large group of scientists is that we had people who covered all of these ranges.

In my absence, the micropaleontologists had been busy. Scott Elias, a fossil insect guy, had been sorting bulk samples of the peat, picking out pieces and parts of insects, and his list of species had begun to grow. He found ground beetles, water scavenger beetles, rove beetles, powder post beetles, dung beetles, bark beetles, leaf beetles, and caddis flies. And he was just getting warmed up.

Charles Nelson is one of our most trusted and committed volunteers.

He is a picker, which means that he takes pans of concentrated debris from screen-washed sediment and picks it for microfossils. This is painstaking work, and Charles can sit essentially motionless for hours, trolling through endless drifts of tiny clods of dirt and fragments of wood, looking for the tiny parts and pieces of small vertebrate animals. For him, a good day might mean that he found two salamander vertebrae and a mouse femur. Charles had been taking samples of sediment from the big mammal skulls, screening the sediment through a window screen, and finding salamander bones, fish jaws, garter snake vertebrae, and parts of a mouse we couldn't identify. His whole haul could fit in a thimble, but that didn't discourage him at all.

Tom Ager, an expert on microscopic plant parts from the U. S. Geological Survey, distilled sediment into a concentrated organic ooze, which he spread on a microscope slide that he then searched for pollen and spore grains. These suckers really are small, often only 20 or 30 microns wide. A thousand microns are in 1 millimeter, or 25,400 microns in 1 inch. That means that Tom was hunting for, finding, and identifying specks that were one one-thousandth of an inch in diameter. Amazingly, these tiny grains are often quite distinctive and immediately tell Tom what sort of plant they come from. Tom can literally take a lump of mud, wash out the sediment, spread the ooze, and begin reading out the names of forest trees, shrubs, and herbs. His very first sample yielded spruce, fir, oak, pine, and Douglas fir.

Beetles, mice, and pollen are not quite as sexy as mammoths and giant bison, but when it comes to fleshing out the picture of what this place looked like, they did their part.

Meanwhile, Kit and I had started talking about the details of the spring dig. Who would provide site security? How would we lead tours? What would happen in the case of cost overruns? What if we couldn't finish digging in time? I had my own questions. How many people did I need? Where was I going

Left: Small bone picking. *Right:* Fossil tiger salamander limb bones, vertebrae, and toes from the pith cavity of a mastodon tusk.

RECONSTRUCTING WHOLE PLANTS FROM FOSSIL BITS

Plants fall apart both in life and death. In life, plants lose their leaves, and their branches break off and re-grow. Their flowers or cones grow, produce seeds or pollen, and then they fall off. Pollen and seeds are carried off by wind, water, insects, birds, and mammals. Since plants have evolved to fall apart, their parts disassociate throughout the plant's life. Compare this to an animal, which in life does not want to lose limbs or flesh, and even in death is held together by muscle and sinew. The fact that plants fall apart presents a very special problem to the paleobotanist (fossil-plant scientist) who is trying to reconstruct and study ancient and sometimes extinct plants. When botanists set out to identify a living plant, they encounter the whole organism with all of its parts intact. As a result, study of living plants is facilitated by a complete set of physical characteristics as well as the plant's DNA. When paleobotanists find a fossil plant, they usually find scattered parts. Except in rare instances, the paleobotanist cannot put the botanical Humpty Dumpty back together again. And this makes it really difficult, but not impossible, to study extinct plants and ecosystems.

In the ancient Snowmastodon lake, we found leaves, pollen, cones, seeds, wood, and parts of flowers. To reconstruct these plants, we identify the particular plant part, figure out what group of plants or what particular plant it goes with, and then look at living examples of those plants to get an idea of the entire organism. Fortunately, almost all plant species we encountered in the ancient lake are still alive today. One of the curious things about this site is that many of its big animal species are extinct, while many of its plant species still live in the Rocky Mountains.

Small tree trunk showing branch arrangement

Waternymph seeds
Najas flexilis

Spruce cones
Picea sp.

Rocky Mountain fir cones
Abies lasiocarpa

Sedge leaves
Cyperaceae

Peat moss
Sphagnum sp.

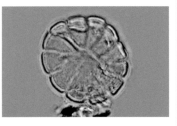

Bladderwort pollen
Utricularia sp.

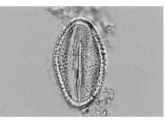

Willow pollen
Salix sp.

Buckbean pollen
Menyanthes sp.

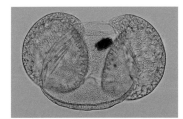

Fir pollen
Abies sp.

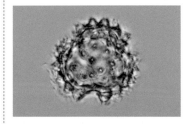

Jacob's ladder pollen
Polemonium sp.

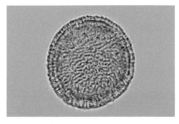

Aster pollen
Aster sp.

to house them, and who was going to feed them? How could I keep track of so many people, and how could we make sure that we didn't screw up the data that we would collect? We also realized that it was important to make sure Roaring Fork Valley locals got a chance to dig. Jodi, Ian, and I burrowed into these questions and made long lists of what we needed to figure out.

We wrote grant proposals to the National Geographic Society and to the National Science Foundation seeking funding for the project, and we kept working the budget. By December 14, I had come to the gruesome conclusion that I was looking at a million-dollar project. This was rapidly growing into a big deal. It seemed possible that we could turn the public interest in the project into financial support, but it wasn't immediately clear how.

One thing we knew was that the discovery mammoth needed a nickname. While we were at the site, everyone seemed to have a different name for the skeleton. Some people were calling it Ziggy, after the Zieglers. Kent Olson had a cute little three-year-old girl named Ella, and that seemed like a sweet name for a young female mammoth. Other people wanted to call it the Snowmammoth or Snowmass Mammoth. We kind of liked the ring of Samammoth after Samantha Richards, our tireless educator who had hauled the bones to all of the students.

Finally, our marketing team decided to name the skeleton through an online vote. On December 16, we offered up five names: Samammoth, Ziggy, Snowy, Jesse, and Ella. More than 15,000 people voted over the next four weeks, and when the votes were counted, Snowy won by a landslide. In addition to the formal vote, we decided to name a few of the other critters as well. We named the bison Jesse to honor Jesse Steele, the deer, Kit to honor Kit Hamby, and the sloth Ziggy, in memory of Timmy Ziegler, the youngest of the Ziegler children who had died in his 30s.

While Snowy was being named, our conservators were trying to dry her bones out in a safe way. All the bones that came down from Snowmass were really wet. We knew that this could lead to mold if we didn't dry them quickly enough, but if we dried them out too fast they would likely warp and crack. Our conservators, led by Jude Southward, normally work in a small lab hidden back in the recesses of the museum. This remote outpost of museology rarely receives visitors, but this changed when the bones came. The lab was buried in bones and tusks, and curious visitors were crowded into the tiny space. Despite all the attention the bones were receiving, I felt pretty comfortable knowing that they were in the hands of trained specialists.

If the bones were in plaster jackets or if they were still covered with dirt, they went to the paleontology preparation lab, where preparators Bryan Small and Heather Finlayson and their staff of volunteers set about cleaning and gluing. My daily tour would always include a stop in the lab, where new treasures emerged every day.

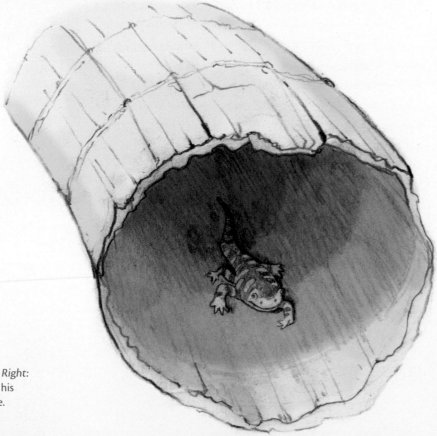

Left: The Snowy logo. *Right:* A tiger salamander in his cylindrical ivory home.

By now, we had determined that the deer-like mammal was, in fact, a deer, but we hadn't collected enough measurements to know if it was an extinct species or the still-living mule deer. The skeleton that we found in the peat was in a large plaster jacket. Bryan assigned volunteers Mike and Liz Lacey the delicate task of cracking open the jacket and exposing the crushed deer. It was amazing to watch the nearly complete skeleton emerge as they carefully scraped away the encasing peat. Both antlers were present but had been badly crushed when Jesse's D6 dozer ran over the skeleton. Mike and Liz worked on this jigsaw puzzle, and bit by tiny bit, the antlers started to emerge from the crush of tiny shards. This was a professional, three-dimensional, virtuoso jigsaw puzzle performance, and anyone who watched it came away not only impressed by the salvage of the magnificent fossils but also by the incredible harmony of this couple. By January, they had logged more than 300 hours of work and they were just beginning to make progress on the deer skeleton jigsaw puzzle (as of this writing, the Laceys have spent more than 700 hours reconstructing this remarkable fossil).

Many of the ivory tusks we brought back had fairly complete pith cavities. These are the cone-shaped tapering openings at the base of the tusk where it attached to the skull of the mastodon or mammoth. We had found a number of loose mastodon tusks in the bottom of the big pit, and we had wrapped these in plastic sheeting to retard their drying. Now

Left: Liz and Mike Lacey working diligently on the partially crushed deer skeleton. *Right:* After hundreds of hours and lots of glue, the antlers of the Snowmass deer begin to look recognizable.

they lay on tables in the conservation lab inside a protective plastic "tusk tent." As volunteers cleaned sediment from the pith cavities, we were amazed to see that they were full of tiny salamander bones. We figured out that the salamanders were living in the tusks that had fallen out of the skulls of the dead mastodons before the tusks were buried in the lake bottom. This was one of the first signs of actual ecology that we were able to observe. I loved the idea of salamanders living in beautiful cylindrical ivory castles, and it didn't take too much thought to start comparing these ancient ivory homes with the modern and mega-opulent homes that line the hillsides of the Roaring Fork Valley today.

Ice Ages and Skiing
SATURDAY, JANUARY 1—MONDAY, JANUARY 31, 2011

On January 23, George Sparks and I drove to Snowmass Village to begin our efforts to meet people in the valley, understand the political landscape, make friends, connect with the press, look for land mines, and find people who would be willing to help us raise the funds we would need when the dig resumed. It was an action-packed two days of back-to-back appointments, coffee stops, and meals. We spent a lot of time driving back and forth between Aspen and Snowmass Village and came to see the connections and tensions that bind the two towns.

It was obvious that the single most important connection was the Aspen Skiing Company, which operates the ski mountains of both towns. Owned by the Crown family from Chicago, the company is managed by a bunch of young, healthy executives who live in the Roaring Fork Valley and know that they have the best jobs on the planet. For several years, I had been watching the Aspen Skiing Company because of their stance on global warming issues. They are not dummies, and they know that one of the first victims of regional global warming is alpine snow and the length of time that it lingers on the slopes. It doesn't take a lot of reasoning to understand that skiing in Colorado would be one of the first losers if temperatures continued to climb. I could see that Ziegler Lake's fossil record of ancient climate had tremendous potential to tell the story of climate

READING THE TUSKS OF MAMMOTHS & MASTODONS

by Daniel Fisher

Although they may not look like it, tusks of elephants, mammoths, and mastodons are teeth that grow a little bit every day of the animal's life. Laid down in daily layers, the tusks of elephants and their extinct kin contain growth rings similar to those of a tree. And just like a tree, you can study the animal's age and life history from its growth rings.

Although both tusks and trees have growth rings, they differ in an important way. Trees add new wood on the outside of previously formed wood, increasing the tree's girth and height, whereas tusks grow by adding cone-shaped layers of ivory to the inside of the tusk base, deep within the socket in which the tusk is held. New cones of ivory extend the length of the tusk (think of stacking pointed ice cream cones), but at its base, not at its tip. Cutting both trees and tusks cross-wise reveals a pattern of concentric layers representing years, but because they grow differently, they must be interpreted differently. With trees, it only takes one cross-wise cut, near the base, to intersect all the annual rings and count how many years the tree lived. In contrast, one such cut on a tusk shows only the cones in that part of the stack. To see all the years in a tusk on one surface, you need to cut it length-wise, intersecting the entire stack of ivory cones.

What makes years show up in trees and tusks? For trees, conditions of growth are most favorable in spring and summer, allowing rapid growth and production of large wood cells. In fall and winter, growth slows down, and trees produce smaller wood cells. The couplet formed by concentric sets of large and small wood cells marks one ring and the passage of one year in the life of the tree. Tusks also grow more quickly in spring and summer, when food is abundant and animals are healthy, and more slowly during the fall and winter, when food is scarce. In this case, an ivory couplet comprised of zones of rapid and slow growth marks the passage of one year of an animal's life.

Within each year, tusks (unlike trees) have layers marking intervals of about two weeks (in mastodons; mammoths have weekly layers) and still finer layers marking days. Measuring the fraction of the last year recorded in ivory tells you what time of year it was when an animal died. In tusks of juveniles, there is a strongly marked layer that records the physiological transition associated with birth, and by tracing seasons and years following this event, we can reconstruct the season of birth, which was usually early spring. Compositional changes following birth let us determine how long a calf nursed from its mother. Later changes in the rate of tusk growth mark sexual maturation in young adults, calving in adult females, and onset of musth (the breeding season) in adult males. In addition to normal events of growth and reproduction, the tusk record has the potential to reveal times of relative hardship or abundance, showing up as slow or rapid growth, respectively, often with compositional clues on the causes of good times or bad. We can even use tusks to tell if typical seasons of death and reproductive schedules changed significantly after humans arrived in North America. This approach shows promise for testing whether human hunting or climate change was a more important cause of mastodon and mammoth extinction. Although the animals themselves are long gone, the life histories of individual mammoths and mastodons are preserved in the ivory autobiographies that we know as tusks.

Above: Cut-away of a tusk root showing concentric ivory rings, with colors added for contrast. *Below:* A small tusk from a young animal showing ivory growth rings.

THIS COLORED LAYER INDICATES A YEAR IN THE LIFE OF THE MASTODON

in the Colorado Rockies, and that story would be relevant to this community.

Only after this visit did I understand that Snowmass ski area styled itself to be the most family-friendly of the local ski mountains. After watching the immense popularity of the *Ice Age* movies (try googling "ice age") and seeing the kids at our ice age festivals in Snowmass Village and Denver, I realized that ice age animals were as compelling to kids as dinosaurs, something I didn't expect.

I could see how the Aspen ski areas could capitalize on the climate aspect of the discovery while Snowmass Mountain could use the big extinct animals to engage kids and families. The whole valley was starting to seem like an ice age theme park with tailor-made audiences already in place.

We stayed at the beautiful new Viceroy Hotel on our visit to Snowmass Village. Built at the foot of the Snowmass ski area, this property anchored the Base Village development that had recently gone belly up as a result of the recession. It was the peak of the ski season, yet the hotel was relatively empty. Likewise, Base Village was more like a place waiting to open than one that was open for business. This was a big difference from Aspen, where the town was bustling with business.

George thought about this, and about the serendipity of the Snowmastodon discovery less than a mile from the mall at Snowmass Village, and said, "It's like the Martians chose to land here and give the town a gift."

On our last night in town, we met our first Ziegler. People had told us that the Zieglers were a quiet and private family that mainly lived in Wisconsin. Most folks we'd talked to had never met a Ziegler. But given the property ownership, we knew we needed to open direct lines of communication with the family so that they were completely comfortable with what we were planning to do. When Snowmass Water and Sanitation acquired the property from the Zieglers to expand the reservoir, they acquired only the land that would be submerged below the water of the reservoir. The Zieglers maintained ownership of all the surrounding property. Water and San was granted an easement to access the reservoir site to build and maintain the reservoir and nothing else. The completed reservoir would be closed to the public, and the Zieglers would in effect have a private lake even though the water in the lake would be owned by the people of Snowmass Village. All this information reinforced the widespread perception that the Zieglers were tough negotiators.

I had spoken to Peter Ziegler, one of Doug's sons, by phone at the end of December, and he was extremely polite but relatively reserved and cautious with his language. It was clear that he was a member of a family that made its decisions together and that he would not make anything that even sniffed of a commitment over the phone.

So it was with curiosity and caution that we approached our meal with Cherrie Catlin, the eldest of the six adult Ziegler children. Cherrie and her husband, Tom, met us at a burger bar in Base Village, and we sat down at a cozy table. They were open and warm, and conversation flowed easily. We

had a complete blast, and by the end of the meal both George and I felt that we had two new friends. That was not how I expected the evening to roll, but it was just another example of how lucky the entire discovery had been. If the rest of the Zieglers were anything like Cherrie, it was going to be a pleasure getting to know them. I felt a huge weight lift from my shoulders since this was one of the last big unknowns about the dig. We headed back to Denver the next day feeling that the whole project was coming together nicely.

Things moved pretty swiftly over the next few weeks. We hired Krista Williams to serve as the administrator for the dig. Knowing that she would have to move to Snowmass Village for the whole spring dig, she post-poned her wedding, which had been scheduled for May. Richard Stucky, our curator of fossil mammals, took the giant bison skull to a nearby Kaiser Permanente clinic to be CAT-scanned. We prepared a careful budget and confirmed that the 2011 effort would be much larger than the 2010 dig. The executive committee of the museum's board gave their final approval, authorizing us to raise and spend up to $1.03 million for the complete project. We finalized our agreement with Snowmass Water and Sanitation, agreeing to begin our dig on May 15 and complete it by July 1, a total of 51 days. This schedule would allow Kit to complete his reservoir project by October and satisfy his contractual obligations to the Zieglers.

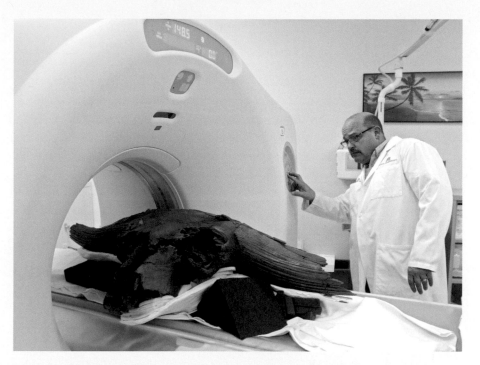

Above: Steve White, from Kaiser Permanente, CAT-scanning the skull of the giant Snowmass bison. This technique images the interior of the skull. At this time, neither horn had been re-attached. *Below:* Ziegler Reservoir in March. A lot of bones lie beneath this snow and ice.

Mastodon Bones in the Golden Dome
TUESDAY, FEBRUARY 1–THURSDAY, MARCH 31, 2011

Around this time, state Senator Gail Schwartz from Snowmass Village and state Representative Laura Bradford from Palisade proposed Colorado Senate Joint Resolution 18 "Concerning Recognition of the Ice Age Discovery in Snowmass Village." On February 24, we took the mastodon tibia that Dave Gyolai found in November (this was the original Flintstone bone that we were now calling the "Magic Tibia" for its ability to wow crowds), a mastodon tusk, and a mastodon tooth to the Colorado State Capitol and presented them to both the Senate and the House, where the bill was unanimously approved in both chambers. It was one of the few bills in 2011 that received comprehensive bipartisan support. Jesse Steele and the crew from Gould Construction and Snowmass Village town officials were on site to receive kudos from the lawmakers. There was a great sense of pride about the discovery and even a bit of competition. Since Jesse Steele lives in Palisade, Representative Bradford said, "Senator Schwartz may own the dirt of this discovery, but the man comes from my district!" It was deeply satisfying to see fossils appreciated at the state capitol.

Preparing for this day, we worked with Senator Schwartz's staff to make a clear and accurate statement about the true significance of the find. In order to do this with accuracy, we researched other ice age fossil sites in Colorado. The state is endowed with a number of important ice age sites, such as Porcupine Cave near Alma, Lamb Springs near Chatfield Reservoir, the Selby and Dutton sites near Yuma, the Dent site near Longmont, and the Haystack Cave site near Gunnison. It was cool to learn about Colorado's rich ice age fossil record, and it was exciting to learn that Snowmass was a cut above the rest.

While I was searching the scientific literature for earlier discoveries, I came across an amazing coincidence in an issue of *Science* magazine from 1930. A one-page article entitled "Occurrence of Mammoth and Giant Bison in Glacial Moraines in the High Mountains of Colorado" described a site at an elevation of 8,000 feet between Gunnison and Montrose where workmen digging a ditch had found mammoth and bison bones,

Jesse Steele, Rep. Laura Bradford, and Sen. Gail Schwartz speak to a reporter and present a mastodon tusk, tooth, and tibia at the state capitol on February 24.

including the horns of a huge bison. Even more amazing, the article had been written by Harold J. Cook, who was then working at the Colorado Museum of Natural History (the original name of the Denver Museum of Nature & Science). None of our museum records had alerted us to this discovery. It turned out that the bison had not been salvaged. We were going to do a better job this time.

After our moment in the sun at the state capitol, the Ice Age Discovery Committee from Snowmass (also called the "Tusk Force") arrived in Denver. Their goal was to see the fossils and, working with the museum, create a strategic plan for responding to this huge opportunity. Many people thought that Snowmass should build a museum to display the recent findings. The Tusk Force came to Denver to explore this idea and to see how a museum operates. We had a great brainstorming session and laid the groundwork for how the committee would function. Personally, I liked the idea of carving new ski runs on Snowmass Mountain in the shape of giant tusks.

With the dig dates in hand, Jodi, Krista, Carol, Ian, and I set about planning and organizing the second phase of the project. We knew we only had 51 days to complete the dig, and we didn't want to miss a beat. We decided to organize the excavation into seven one-week segments and

staff each week separately. With Ian and me as joint commanders of the entire field operation, we would appoint a team of field captains who would each oversee a team of five to eight diggers. Krista was in charge of organizing the finances, tracking the comings and goings of the people, and coordinating the food, supplies, and lodging. Ian was in charge of the logistics of the excavation and ordering or renting tools, equipment, vehicles, and supplies. Carol organized the teams responsible for the data collection and collection management. Meghan McFarlane from the conservation lab would be in charge of conservation and specimen photography. Shelley Thompson coordinated our fund-raising activities. Jodi coordinated our complex outreach effort, which included school visits in the Roaring Fork Valley, lectures, festivals in Denver and Snowmass, our Scientists-In-Action broadcasts from the site to classrooms, and the National Geographic television show. The museum had agreed to build a small exhibit on the Snowmass Village Mall, and Jodi led that project as well. Gannon Kashiwa led a team that was responsible for filming and documenting the dig. Heather Hope would lead the media and public relations team. Ian and I coordinated the scientific core team that managed the 37 project scientists.

The Magic Tibia has its day in the Colorado House of Representatives.

Then we set about recruiting our teams of diggers. We knew that our trained volunteer staff was champing at the bit to be part of the dig, so we hosted a big meeting in the IMAX theater to explain what we were looking for and who was eligible to apply. It was an amazing night, as more than 200 people turned out to learn about how they might help with the dig. Based on our experience in the fall, we emphasized the difficulty of the dig: the slippery mud, the high elevation, the extreme weather, and the endless shoveling. We wanted to scare people so that only the truly hardy would apply. Our volunteer office helped process the applications. We gave first priority to volunteers who had been trained in our two-decade-old paleontology certification course.

We also knew that we wanted to involve Roaring Fork locals in the excavation and realized that we could get the best long-term impact if we chose educators who would be able to parlay their experiences at the dig with ongoing education in the valley. We created applications and distributed them via the newspapers in the Roaring Fork Valley.

We also decided that we needed a team of nine college interns whom we could count on for the entire seven-week dig, so we sent out applications and inquiries to universities around the country.

Meanwhile, up in Snowmass, Kit was planning the construction project and figuring out how we would fit into it. Much to the disappointment of Mark Gould and his staff, Hudick Excavating Inc. of Castle Rock won the bid for the reservoir construction. This meant that Jesse Steele, Kent Olson, and other key players from the fall, would not be part of the spring dig. Initially, we thought that Snowmass Village would coordinate the security at the site and run public tours. But due to safety issues, we realized that we couldn't do tours, and site security reverted back to Kit and his team.

Krista and Carol started ordering and stockpiling supplies. On one memorable day, $5,000 worth of snacks arrived at the loading dock. I had never seen so many potato chips in one place in my life.

We were now spending in earnest, and we began to ramp up our fund-raising efforts with the hope of raising money as fast as we spent it. Shelley

Thompson coordinated parties in the homes of several DMNS supporters in Aspen, Snowmass Village, and Denver. At these events, George and I presented the amazing story of the discovery and asked the attendees to help us figure out how to finance the massive effort. George, Shelley, and I also visited community leaders in the Roaring Fork Valley to tell them about the project and get their advice about how we could do the best possible job on behalf of the valley. We met with folks from the Aspen Skiing Company, Aspen Center for Environmental Studies, Aspen Historical Society, Snowmass Tourism, Anderson Ranch, *Aspen Daily News*, *The Aspen Times*, *Snowmass Sun*, Aspen Chamber of Commerce, Aspen Institute, Aspen Community Foundation, Aspen Science Center, Aspen and Snowmass Rotary, and the Town of Snowmass Village. It was a crash course in local politics. We did not want to miss a beat once we got back to the business of digging.

Our secret weapon, Ian's mom, Liz Miller, had been the central figure of our logistical success in the fall. She ended up liking Snowmass so much that she and her husband, Jim, moved there from Grand Junction. Liz got a job as a ski instructor on the mountain and became one of our ears on the ground as the planning progressed.

From day one back in October, the Roaring Fork Valley media had reported the dig on an almost daily basis. In Aspen, an old-time newspaper war was going on between *The Aspen Times* and the *Aspen Daily News*, with the result that we were often front-page news. I was surprised how often people would recognize me on the streets of Aspen and Snowmass Village and yell, "Hey, aren't you the mammoth guy?"

On March 22, the Aspen Historical Society hosted an evening event at the Silvertree Hotel in Snowmass Village. I was scheduled to give a talk about the discoveries to date and our plans for the upcoming spring dig. By the time I arrived from Denver, a crowd of more than 700 people assembled. The Roaring Fork Valley had a raging case of mammoth fever.

Ian's mom, Liz Miller, points out Ziegler Reservoir with the tip of her ski pole.

Bring It On
FRIDAY, APRIL 1–THURSDAY, MAY 12, 2011

On April 1, Ian ran into my office waving a copy of the *Aspen Daily News*. On the cover was the headline, "Mastodon finds exposed as mammoth fraud: Daunting craftsmanship of tiny salamander penises, other more massive bones fooled now-disgraced scientists." The article went on to quote, "'Career'sssover,' slurred Dr. Kirk Wood to a reporter who found the scientist and a mostly empty bottle of gin outside the spot where it turns out the items were planted." Ian was in a bit of a panic until I reminded him of the date.

As we moved around the valley, we learned that locals were already capitalizing on the discovery. Mammoth burgers showed up at local eateries; mammoth and mastodon T-shirts were appearing in store windows; and People's Press, an Aspen-based publishing house, announced that it would shortly be publishing a book by local author Amiee White Beazley entitled, *Snowmastodon! Snow Day Adventure*. That one really caught us by surprise, as we had been discussing making a children's book about the discovery ourselves and here was one scheduled to be published before

we had even finished the dig. The locals really were starting to take ownership of the discovery.

Chris Faison, a teacher at the Aspen Community School near Woody Creek, e-mailed me to let me know that he and his class of first-graders had built a life-sized cardboard mammoth. This I had to see for myself, so I drove to the school and slipped into the main room just as the school was in assembly. Sure enough, Faison and his kids had fabricated a properly proportioned male mammoth. He told me that he had assigned a bone to each kid and they had worked at home with their parents to fabricate their portion of the big beast.

While Chris was teaching his kids about mammoths, our school outreach team was making good on the promise that I had made to Kit, to visit Roaring Fork Valley schools and educate the kids about the discovery. Ian had worked with a team of our educators to create an assembly program called *Time Scene Investigation*. Aimed at elementary school kids, the program was based around a huge screen that looked like a giant smart phone, called the iStone. Our educator-actors used it to call back in time to speak with Maury the Mastodon, Snowy the Mammoth, a grumpy old *Tyrannosaurus rex*, and Ian the Curator. The program was really delightful to watch. A group of our museum educator-actors then delivered the program 62 times in 20 schools, to a total of 6,381 kids in the Roaring Fork Valley.

Our logistics team came up to Snowmass for one last pre-dig visit on the weekend of April 8. We interviewed nearly 50 local educators for 15 coveted spots on the dig team. Meeting the teachers and seeing their passion for the project was terrific. We wanted to accept them all, but we already had a nearly full list of qualified workers.

I had one last thing to do before heading back to Denver. Doug Ziegler was in town for his 84th birthday, and his whole family had assembled for

Top left: Illustrator Paul Antonson and local author Amiee White Beazley imagined their own Snowmastodon story. *Below left:* Chris Faison at Aspen Community School worked with a team of school kids to build a life-sized cardboard mammoth. *Below right:* Jill Katzenberger presents the *Time Scene Investigation* school program using a huge iStone.

the first time in several years. I talked to Cherrie and Peter, who invited me to give a presentation to the entire Ziegler clan. I knew that it was important that the Zieglers, particularly Doug Ziegler, embrace the idea of the excavation and its significance. We had named the sloth after Timmy Ziegler, and I wanted to make sure that they would take the sloth name as a compliment and an appropriate memorial of their lost son and brother.

I stood in front of their fireplace and spoke to the Zieglers for more than an hour about the discovery and why it was so significant for the town, the valley, and the state. They peppered me with questions about the fossils, the dig, and my funding sources. They wanted my assurance that our work wouldn't delay the completion of the dam. I learned that they considered themselves stewards of the land and were truly concerned about conserving this amazing piece of property that they had owned since 1958. I had just returned from Seattle, where I was a speaker at an event in honor of Estella Leopold, one of the early pioneers in the study of fossil pollen and the youngest daughter of the famed ecologist Aldo Leopold. It turned out that the Zieglers were from Slinger, Wisconsin, close to where Aldo Leopold had built the now-famous shack where he wrote *A Sand County Almanac*. Peter Ziegler and his wife, Joan, were active in the Aldo Leopold Society. I left the meeting knowing that we stood on common ground and feeling that I had won the trust of the family. Everything was now in place for the dig to begin.

In late April, I got a call from Mark Gould's assistant and Kent Olson's wife, Wendi. Apparently one of Gould's workers had found a tooth in stockpiled peat that Gould's team had hauled away from the site back in October. Wendi was coming to Denver and she wanted to drop the tooth off so I could identify it. Based on the photos she emailed me, it looked like it might be something new for the site. It turned out to be a perfect molar of an ice age camel, the sixth large mammal species for the Snowmass site. This discovery may come as a big surprise to people who think camels are desert animals, but camels are actually some of the more common ice age mammals found in Colorado and are often found with mammoths.

More than a year earlier, Ian and I had made a plan to raft through the Grand Canyon with a bunch of friends, and now that time had come. On April 27, we departed for a 15-day river trip from Lee's Ferry to Lake Mead. The walls of the Grand Canyon are eye candy for a geologist, and we were surprised to see caves in the limestone that were full of fossilized giant sloth dung. Even though the animals had been extinct for more than 13,000 years, the desert climate had preserved their dung as if it had been dropped last year. Everywhere we went, our attention was directed back to Snowmass. The trip gave us plenty of time to contemplate the seven grueling weeks of digging that would greet us when we returned. People who have floated the Colorado through the Grand Canyon know that it tends to fill your mind with big thoughts and aspirations. It was a fine way to get ready for the biggest dig in the museum's history.

ICE AGE CAMEL
Camelops sp.

The molar of an ice age camel was an unexpected find in a pile of peat from Ziegler Reservoir.

ICE AGE HISTORY OF THE ROARING FORK VALLEY

Over the last 2 million years, glaciers in the Rocky Mountains carved valleys and cirques, dredged lakes, bulldozed mountains of boulders and sand, and ground peaks into muddy debris. In fact, most recent research on mountain glaciers suggests that they are the most powerful erosive force on Earth and play a major role in limiting the height of mountain ranges. The glacial buzz saw theory argues that as mountains increase in height, they block more clouds and create more precipitation. With an increase in altitude, rain turns to snow and glaciers grow on the mountain slopes. Since the glaciers are so effective at erosion, the mountains can only get so high. If the glaciers erode too much, the mountains become too low to cause snow. As a result, many mountain ranges with glaciers are thought to be in a balance between glacier growth and mountain height. The glaciers of the Colorado Rockies and the Roaring Fork Valley have waxed and waned with the global oscillation between cold glacial and warmer interglacial events. The result is a buzz saw that is regularly turning on and off.

Even though it is likely that more than 20 glacial events have occurred in the Rockies, only the two most recent ones have left evidence of their existence behind in the Roaring Fork Valley. These are the Bull Lake and Pinedale glaciations, which reached their peaks about 140,000 and 21,000 years ago, respectively. These names are regional designations for the Illinoian and Wisconsin glaciations, which occurred throughout North America. The evidence for earlier episodes of glaciations were wiped out by these two most recent episodes. The warm period between the Illinoian (Bull Lake) and Wisconsin (Pinedale) glaciations is known as the Sangamon interglacial.

Evidence from the most recent Pinedale glaciation is everywhere in the Roaring Fork Valley. The beautiful U-shaped valleys of Snowmass and Maroon Creeks, the flat outwash plains of the lower Roaring Fork near Carbondale, and the high mountain lakes dotting the mountains are all glacial features that show that the valley was very recently packed with ice. We can tell by the shape of gravel ridges in the upper valley that Aspen was entirely under ice 21,000 years ago. Even though most of the glacial features in the Roaring Fork Valley are Pinedale in age, we also know that the Pinedale glaciation was less extreme than the Bull Lake. This very fact led to the preservation of the Snowmastodon site. A Bull Lake glacier in the Snowmass Creek Valley pushed up over the ridge above Snowmass Village and bulldozed a 30-acre bowl at the top of the ridge. When the glacier melted, the bowl filled with water, forming the glacial Ziegler Lake. Over the ensuing years, the lake filled with windblown silt, logs, and bones. Since the glacier that refilled Snowmass Creek during the Pinedale time was smaller than its Bull Lake predecessor, it did not push over the ridgetop, and it did not destroy the ridgetop lake.

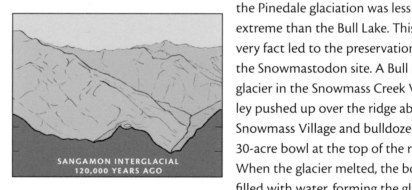

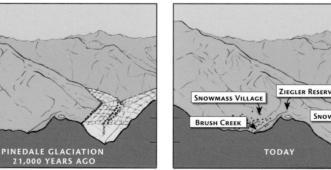

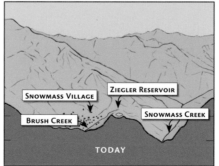

BULL LAKE GLACIATION
130,000 YEARS AGO

SANGAMON INTERGLACIAL
120,000 YEARS AGO

PINEDALE GLACIATION
21,000 YEARS AGO

TODAY

SNOWMASS VILLAGE · ZIEGLER RESERVOIR · SNOWMASS CREEK · BRUSH CREEK

These four diagrams show how a glacier flowing down the Snowmass Creek valley formed the Glacial Lake Ziegler, and how a later glacier was not large enough to destroy it. These two facts make this site unique and explain why it has such a long fossil record.

Glacial Lake Ziegler was formed when a glacier flowing down Snowmass Creek valley advanced over the valley wall, pushing a lobe of glacial moraine to the head of the Brush Creek drainage. This painting shows the receding glacier about 130,000 years ago, after it has formed the moraine but before it has fully melted away.

During the Sangamon interglacial, Glacial Lake Ziegler was 35 feet deep and surrounded by a diverse conifer forest. On a pleasant summer day about 120,000 years ago a mature male Jefferson's ground sloth surveys the view (right foreground), while in the middle distance, a large female *Bison latifrons* grazes on grass and two American mastodons browse on foliage (left middle).

About 70,000 years ago, glaciers once again began to fill the Snowmass Creek valley. Glacial Lake Ziegler had filled in to become a sedge marsh. A male Columbian mammoth grazes in the foreground. Two female mule deer (left) are alert while a few camels graze (right).

July 15, 2012: Ziegler Reservoir is once again a small lake surrounded by aspen. The large bear that visited the excavation in June 2011, surveys his domain.

ACT THREE

Loadin' and Goin'
FRIDAY, MAY 13–SATURDAY, MAY 14, 2011

We had agreed with Kit Hamby that we would dig from May 15 to July 1. By May 13, we were as ready as we were going to be. We had hired nine interns to work alongside the museum staff for the entire seven-week dig. In contrast, most of the volunteers would work for only one week of the seven. This way we hoped to have a steady flow of fresh diggers. This also meant that we were keeping track of more than 200 people. We were awash in all of these names, so I decided that I would number the interns based on the order of their arrival. I collected Intern #1 at Denver International Airport and took her straight to the museum to show her the fossils from the fall's dig. The lab staff had re-assembled the massive *Bison latifrons* skull, and it was a sight to behold. Corinna Troll had just graduated from Bard College in New York, where she had completed a research project on cores from an ice age lake in the Great Basin. This warmed her to the charms of the ice ages, and she already knew me because of my long collaboration with her dad, Ray.

The rest of the team was busily loading a fleet of vehicles and preparing to drive to Snowmass the next day. We had benefited greatly from the luxury of six months of planning, and we hoped that we had thought of everything. Ian and I were assigned the roles of official tweeters and were up and running on Twitter under the names of @iandigs and @leafdoctor. The hash tag #iceagedig posted our tweets directly to the museum's website. We had discussed the matter with Kit and his crew and had decided that unlike in the fall, the dig site would not be open to the public or to the press except for two specific press tours. We would issue press releases with photos on Tuesdays and releases with video on Fridays. And we would tweet like birds.

On Saturday morning I loaded up Big Blue and picked up Richard Stucky at his house. Richard had hired me back in 1990, and we had worked together to build the exhibit. In recent years, we hadn't spent much time together, so we had a great talk as we drove west on I-70. We stopped in

Corinna Troll's arm span is no match for the 6 foot 4 inch *Bison latifrons* skull.

Carbondale for a lovely lunch with friends and finally pulled into Snowmass Village around 4 p.m.

In the fall we had stayed at the Top of the Village and loved it so much that we moved our entire operation there in the spring. Ian and about a dozen team members were already there when Richard and I arrived. Intern #2 was Lesley Petrie, a chipper and friendly woman who had just graduated from the University of Southern California. A native of Black Hawk, one of Colorado's gambling towns, Lesley is a delightful mixture of L.A. smarts and Colorado mountain town charm. I unloaded the truck and moved into a large three-bedroom condo with a view up the slopes. We gathered the initial group of 14 for our first orientation.

Safety was a major concern. We knew that with more than 200 diggers, we would have ample opportunity for accidents, and a serious one could ruin the entire effort. I appointed Ian as the safety officer, and he memorized the official project HASP (Health and Safety Plan). That night he led us in a dreadfully boring and excruciatingly long recitation of all of the ways that we could get hurt.

By mid-May, snow and ice covered much of Ziegler Reservoir and more snow was to come.

Week One: Snow and Ice
SUNDAY, MAY 15—SATURDAY, MAY 21, 2011

The next morning when I hopped in the shower, the water was ice cold. No problem, this condo had three bathrooms. I hopped in the second shower and found the hot water I was looking for. After showering, I reached out to grab a towel and before I knew it, my legs were above my head and I came down with a slurpy smack, bisecting my hip on the raised steel rim of the glass door frame. I lay there motionless for a few moments, trying to take stock of what had just happened. There was a large, angry bruise and a bloody cut on the side of my thigh, and I realized that nothing in the HASP had prepared me for this.

With warm and sunny weather, the previous week's snow was starting to melt. The deep hole from last fall had filled with more than 20 feet of water and ice over the winter. Kit started pumping out the water in April, so by the time we arrived the hole was still covered with snow and ice, but only about six feet of water sat in the deepest part of the excavation that we called the sump. We all brought tall rubber boots and rubberized rain gear, which was a good thing because the entire site was a muddy quagmire. Within minutes we all experienced the same sticky mud that had

trapped Snowy. It was a hilarious first day as we slowly moved around the site, getting stuck and helping others get unstuck.

We shoveled snow and tried to reorient ourselves to the site that we had known so well six months ago. We had covered Snowy's excavation with tarps and dirt so it could survive the winter, and it required a couple hours of shoveling to find the mud that covered the tarp.

Carol Lucking, the data captain, was in charge of locality numbers and working the surveying devices. Meghan McFarlane, one of the museum's conservators, was the bone-washing captain in charge of receiving the bones from the field, checking their labels, washing them, and photographing each one. Working in a small concrete room at the Snowmass Water and Sanitation District offices, she had to walk past large tanks of aerating sewage to get to her work space. Our preparators, Bryan Small and Heather Finlayson, and Ian's brother Dane were digging captains. Each captain was assigned an intern.

On Monday, Intern #3 arrived. Kaitlin Stanley was a recent Colorado State University graduate, where she had worked with our sloth specialist Greg McDonald. Strawberry blonde and freckled just like Intern #1, Kaitlin came equipped with an impressive knowledge of mammalian skeletal anatomy.

Earlier in the spring, we ran a search for a new curator of dinosaurs and had hired a young paleontologist named Joe Sertich, who was just finishing his PhD at Stony Brook University on Long Island. At the time, we figured that dinosaur bones weren't that different from mammoth bones and that Joe might prove to be a big asset on the dig. A big question in his interview was, "What do you think about spending the first two months of this job in a giant mud hole?" His enthusiastic response told us that we had the right guy.

Joe defended his PhD thesis in New York on May 10, hopped in his car, and drove straight to Snowmass Village. He reported for work on May 16. Ian and I gave Joe the third room in our condo (the one with the dangerous shower) so that we could take advantage of the next two months to bring him up to speed on his new role as a museum scientist.

Kit arranged the construction kick-off meeting for Monday morning. Ian and I attended and met with 11 other guys representing six organizations: Snowmass Water and San, two engineering firms (URS and W. W.

Joe Sertich, our new curator of dinosaurs, just showed up for his first day on the job. Big mammals for the next 50 days.
#iceagedig
17 May

Wheeler Inc.), the state engineer's office, the Colorado Water Conservation Board, and Hudick Excavating Inc. We were all going to have to work together to achieve the dual goals of saving the fossils and completing the reservoir. Joe Enzer delivered another recitation of the HASP. We discussed each group's responsibility, and Ian and I got our first lesson in how a big construction project works. The guys were bemused by the presence of

Opposite left: Ian Miller surveys the ice that had formed on the lake that filled the reservoir over the winter. SWSD had pumped out the water, lowering the sheet of ice onto the top of the fossil-bearing sediment. *Opposite right:* After a few hours of shoveling, we uncovered the tarps that we had left on top of Snowy's excavation in the fall. *Below:* As snow gave way to mud, there wasn't a vehicle on site that could move without getting stuck.

paleontologists, and we could tell that they were trying to size us up and see if we were up to the task. Based on the aggressive dam construction schedule, our 51-day plan was not going to have much flexibility.

On Tuesday, we held a press conference to kick off the dig in the newly opened Ice Age Discovery Center on the Snowmass Village. Jodi and her team back in Denver had done great work transforming a vacated real estate sales office into a sweet little mammoth-themed visitor's center that was to be staffed by volunteers recruited by Snowmass Tourism. Real excitement was in the air, and the public could hardly wait to see what we would find.

Back at the site, what we were mainly finding was mud. The thaw had saturated the ground, and it was impossible to move around on foot in the muck. Joe Enzer ordered us a truckload of wooden pallets to build walkways. When the pallet truck arrived, it sank up to its axles. Kevin Burr fired up a big loader to pull out the truck, and the loader sank in up to its hubs. Finally Kevin was able to use a

track hoe to yank the loader and the pallet truck free. Then the National Geographic Suburban sank up to its axles. It was great fun, but we weren't exactly finding fossils.

National Geographic was getting good footage of stuck vehicles, so Ian and I decided to distract them with a discovery. We were able to make our way to the spot where we had found the Magic Tibia back in November. With a bit of digging through the snow, we located the top of the fossil-bearing debris flow, which we knew to be rich in fossils. I offered Eleanor Grant, the producer, the opportunity to film us finding a fossil. She told us to find a fossil first and then she would film us. That seemed backwards to me, so I told her that I would guarantee we could find a fossil in five minutes or less. Neither she nor the cameraman believed this was possible, but they started rolling the camera. Within four minutes, Ian spotted a bone. At first I thought it was a part of a bison scapula (shoulder blade), but then I realized that it was the radius (forearm bone) of a sloth. We were on the trail of Ziggy!

One of the problems with the sticky clay and slurpy mud was that it was easy to break shovel handles. After a few days we had lots of casualties, so I sent Carol to Glenwood Springs to buy a bunch of better shovels. She loaded a shopping cart with 40 fiberglass-handled shovels and headed for the checkout counter. This turned out to be perfect bait for the handymen of Glenwood, who swarmed her like she was at a singles' bar. Who knew that a cart full of shovels would have that effect? She explained that she had lots of husbands to bury, and that put the boys at bay. The new shovels made a huge difference.

Digging captain Bryan Small had started to remove the clay from the big Clay Mammoth we had found the previous fall. Interns #1, Corinna, and #3, Kaitlin, were helping him. I wandered over and was amazed to see them literally and completely covered in sticky, slimy clay. I had no idea how we would ever get them clean, but I admired their willingness to become mired.

Intern #4, Tyler Kerr, arrived the next day. He had just graduated with a geology degree from Franklin and Marshall College in Lancaster,

Left: National Geographic cameramen film Kirk at the big wall. The layers exposed here are below the mammoth level and above the mastodon level. The yellow layer at thigh level was deposited about 100,000 years ago. *Right:* Interns Kaitlin Stanley and Corinna Troll digging in the sticky clay at the Clay Mammoth excavation.

Pennsylvania. I had given a talk there in April, and Tyler was savvy enough to read up on Snowmastodon before engaging me in conversation. Intern #5, Brittany Grimm, was an undergraduate at Penn State University, where she had impressed Russ Graham with her enthusiasm and curiosity.

Despite the conditions, we were developing a strategy to mine the bones. We dug underneath the debris flow and confirmed Ian's idea that a layer of silt was below it. With the use of a mini-excavator, we cut parallel trenches downhill, isolating big rectangles of debris flow. We called the big rectangles "brownies" because our intention was to scoop them up just like you would scoop a brownie out of a pan. We named each trench so that we knew where we were, and, as in the fall, we pounded steel rebar into the top of each brownie so that we could measure the position of each fossil relative to the numbered rebar, preserving the precise location data for each fossil. Making the trenches required close attention because the mini-excavator had to cut the trench though the fossil-rich debris flow layer (which was about 2 feet thick) to expose the underlying silt.

Kit had allowed us to hire Carlos Mendoza, one of his equipment operators, for the entire dig. Carlos was a deft hand with the mini-excavator, and we rapidly integrated him with our team. A dig captain would stand

in the shallow trench and watch the bucket of the mini-excavator as Carlos scooped. Frequently, the captain would spot a bone and signal to Carlos with a closed fist and a raised arm. Carlos would pause; we would measure the bone, number it, and remove it; and Carlos would keep digging. With his soft touch, Carlos could often tell that he had hit a bone before the captain even saw it. The plan was to use the trenches not only to define the brownies but also as a place where the shovelers could start to chew away at the brownies to find fossils. This method was working pretty well.

Then it started to rain pretty hard. Then the rain turned to sleet, and then the sleet turned to heavy, wet snow. Suddenly it was November 15 all over again.

We decided that we should make the dig into a contest and that each of the digging captains would tally the bones that their teams found. We called it the "No Bone Left Behind Challenge" and filmed an introductory video that named each team. Heather Finlayson was captain of team Tiger Salamander. Dane Miller was captain of Team Trench. Bryan Small was captain of Team Mammoth. And Joe Sertich was captain of Team Sloth. Carol, the data captain, and Meghan, the bone-washing captain, were assigned the job of being impartial judges.

On May 19 we awoke to a winter wonderland. A foot of snow was on the ground, and it was still snowing heavily. People had warned me that May 15 was an ambitious date to start an excavation at an elevation of 8,875 feet in the Rockies, and they were not wrong. We had worked hard for the last five days, so we thought we would take it easy for a day and see if the weather changed. After breakfast, Joe Sertich, Ian, and I went back to our condo and were sitting around watching the snow, relaxing,

Left: Bryan Small gets stuck in the mud while trying to get Heather Finlayson unstuck. *Above:* Carlos Mendoza, our ace mini-excavator operator.

Top: Joe Enzer, the formidable owner's representative for SWSD, was always present on the site, always watching. *Bottom:* Joe Sertich digs around the edge of a big mastodon pelvis.

and drinking coffee when there was a loud knock on the door. In walked Joe Enzer in his field gear, covered with snow. Did I mention that Joe is a mountain of a man? He had come to tell us that we weren't going to find any fossils by sitting in our condo and that we had an awful lot of dirt to move by July 1. He recommended that we get our gear on and get back to the site. We did.

Intern #6, Adam Freierman from Colorado College, was the next to arrive. Ian met Adam in Wyoming the previous summer and had recognized him as a hard worker. Another freckled strawberry blonde, he was known for never wearing shoes on campus. We made him wear boots on the site. He was followed by Intern #7, Brown University student Hannah O'Neill, yet another freckled, strawberry blonde. She worked as a paleontology teen intern with Richard Stucky. Intern #8, Nate Fox, had interned the previous summer at the Mammoth Site in Hot Springs, South Dakota, and came well recommended by Larry Agenbroad. We snapped him right up.

We had initially planned to work six days and rest on the seventh, a Saturday. But a combination of our fear of Joe Enzer and our love of finding fossils led most of us to work in the snow all day Saturday, May 21. It was a cold, sloppy day. George Sparks was digging with us that day. He was working with Nate and Kaitlin near the bottom of one of the brownies when Nate's shovel broke through a thin layer of silt and punched into a void. After some cleaning and inspection, we realized that Nate had punched into the top of a mastodon skull. We could now see that the silt beneath the debris flow was also very rich in bones. About 30 feet away, Joe Sertich was digging in the silt and came across a 4-foot-wide entire mastodon pelvis. Mark Gould, no longer the contractor on the site, had come up from Carbondale to dig with us for a day. He found a splendid mastodon ulna (lower leg bone). The site was yielding bones at a staggering rate, and we were easily able to ignore the miserable digging conditions because of the great fossils.

Ian and Carlos were working on a trench we called "First Blood" when Carlos felt something and backed off. Ian worked for a few moments with a bamboo tool and uncovered an amazing mastodon tusk, maybe 8 inches in diameter. It, too, was in the silt below the debris flow.

That night, George and I drove to Carbondale to present at the Roaring Fork Cultural Council, an evening of conversation organized by Jim Calaway, a well-known local philanthropist. This was a chance for us to spread the news of the dig and let the community know that we had not yet figured out how to fund it. I brought the ulna that Mark Gould found as well as a humerus that we had found later in the day. The two bones fit together in perfect articulation. The format for the evening was for Mark Gould to interview me onstage and then for us to engage the audience of 200 by answering their questions. The two bones lay on the table in front of us. They were still saturated with water from being in the ground less than two hours before. As we talked, the bones drained water off the table and onto the stage. The audience realized that they were seeing an extremely fresh discovery. Our first week was over. We had only six more to meet our deadline.

Week Two: Once-Dug Dirt
SUNDAY, MAY 22—SATURDAY, MAY 28, 2011

Week two saw our first nearly complete crew. We were still missing Intern #9, but our team had grown to 43 diggers and we were killing it. The team captains were getting used to directing the diggers, and the interns were beginning to be useful to the team captains. Our weekly routine was evolving. Sunday would start with a site orientation where I would guide the new diggers around the empty lake bed, showing them all of the main fossil sites: Snowy's grave, the Clay Mammoth, and the various trenches and brownies that were appearing in the big pit. I would tell them of our evolving knowledge of how and when the lake had formed and how the fossils had come to be buried there. By now we were pretty confident that the basin formed during the end of the Bull Lake glaciation, around 130,000 years ago. Because it was on top of a hill, there was no uphill above it, and because its catchment was small, no streams of any size flowed into it. Extrapolating from these observations, we surmised that the sediments that filled the lake came from two distinct sources: landslides from the moraine around the lake edge and airborne dust from the sky.

The airborne dust theory surprised people, but all of them had seen the red dust that routinely appears on Colorado ski slopes, and they were aware that this dust blows in from the red rock country of western Colorado and eastern Utah. The modern example easily made the case. We would test the case later by asking geologists who specialized in windblown sediments to assess the material from the lake and see if our story could be confirmed by laboratory analysis.

A lake that fills with wind-blown dust instead of stream-carried sand is a lake that would take a long time to fill. We surmised that the lake slowly filled between 130,000 and 40,000 years ago, before it eventually became shallow enough that sedges and other water plants could grow even in the middle of the lake, and the lake itself became a shallow marsh. The mastodons lived by the lake early in its history, and Snowy became trapped in the marsh late in the lake's history.

Tony Dicroce digs a drainage trench.

ZIEGLER RESERVOIR TIME LINE

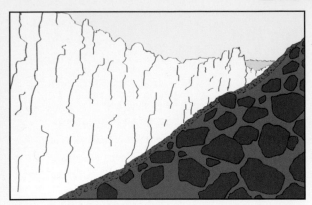

About 130,000 years ago, a glacier forms the future lake basin and fills it with ice. The walls of the basin are the glacier's moraine.

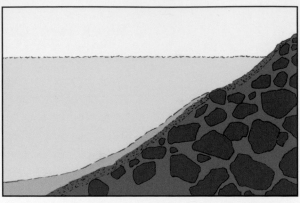

Glacial Lake Ziegler forms when the glacier melted. The lake begins to accumulate windblown silt.

About 120,000 years ago, Glacial Lake Ziegler continues to fill with silt, debris flows, and the bones of mastodons, bison, and sloth.

About 70,000 years ago, the lake fills to the top and becomes a marsh. Mammoths (including Snowy), bison, and deer become trapped in the muddy mire.

Water deepens, transforming the marsh into a shallow lake. The Clay Mammoth is buried during this time.

The lake dries up and becomes the meadow that Doug Ziegler eventually purchased in 1958.

Lake Deborah, formed in 1961 by the construction of a small earthen dam, remains in place until the SWSD excavation begins in September 2010.

By July 2011, the fossil excavation is complete and the dam site is cleaned down to the top of the 130,000-year-old glacial moraine.

By October 2011, the new earthen dam impounds 250 acre-feet of water in a deeper Ziegler Reservoir.

Aerial photograph of Ziegler Reservoir looking down and toward the west. This view shows all of the main excavation sites for fossils and for the dam itself.

Labels visible in the photograph:

- HUDICK TRAILER
- CLAY MAMMOTH DIG SITE
- DMNS TOOL CONTAINER
- DMNS TRAILER
- DMNS LUNCH TENT
- SNOWY DIG SITE
- THE WALL
- PORTALEU DIG SITE
- DMNS DIGGERS
- MINI-EXCAVATOR
- PORTA-POTTIES
- PUMP HOUSE
- LOCATION OF NEW DAM
- BEACH MASTODON DIG SITE

Once I oriented the new diggers to the history of the lake, I gave them the tool lesson. We used two main tools: a shovel and a 6-inch half-round piece of bamboo. The shovel was for digging, and the bamboo was to be used once a bone was found. Digging involved finding rocks, wood, and bone (not quite rock, paper, scissors), and required careful attention to not scar or break the bone. The bamboo tool was soft enough that it wouldn't scratch the bone.

After orientation, I turned the new diggers over to Joe Enzer, who taught them all about site safety. A trailer, which served as our headquarters and a place to store our tools, was also our muster point in case of emergency. Joe told them long and terrifying stories about the dangers of slipping and falling (I would usually insert my shower story at this point), being run down by heavy equipment, sunburn, heat stroke, altitude sickness, self-inflicted shovel wounds, strained backs, crushed toes, sprained ankles, twisted knees, heart attacks, traffic accidents, food poisoning, bears (one had actually wandered past the condos that morning), lightning strikes, indigestion, constipation, and asteroid impacts.

Once trained and appropriately scared, the volunteers were each assigned to one of the dig captains and immediately put to work. On May 22, we had shovel teams working on five separate trenches. Dane Miller led a team that was working just below the 15-foot-tall wall that marked the edge of the dam excavation. The wall, which

Bryan Small uses a bamboo tool to expose the top of a mastodon skull.

had been there since the previous fall, showed an excellent cross section of the lake-filling silt. At the base of the wall was a big flat area of silt. Dane's team cut two parallel east–west trenches and began to carve out a huge brownie. Unlike the area farther east on the dam face, this area turned out to be fairly devoid of bones, and Dane's team dug and dug, occasionally finding a snail, twig, or cone but essentially no bones. Meanwhile, a mere 50 feet away, the teams digging with Joe, Heather, and Bryan were finding bones at a steady clip. By the end of the day, the bone count for the site stood at 103.

Monday, May 23 was a great day, sunny in the morning before it rained. Then it hailed and then rained and then hailed again. Team Tiger Salamander was digging in the First Blood trench, trying to expose the tusk Ian had found. Volunteer Cyrus Green

discovered our first mastodon mandible. Gianna Sullivan, who had arrived to set up our Scientists-In-Action broadcast, was poking around with a piece of bamboo and found the second mastodon skull of the spring.

On Tuesday, Ian and I attended the weekly construction meeting, where we were informed that despite everyone's hard work, we were only moving 25 yards a day and that we would have to increase our daily production to 85 yards if we wanted to completely excavate the site by July 1. By their estimate, we needed to move 4,000 yards to completely clear the dam face. That was a shocking reality, one that made me start to think that we needed to up our game.

We countered with the observation that we had been digging by hand for most of the previous 10 days because the sloppy site conditions had prevented the mini-excavator from accessing our digs. Only in the last few days had Carlos been able to get his machine down to help us by digging the trenches and also by moving the piles we had dug by hand.

Ian and I talked it over and decided to found the religion of "once-dug dirt." Our religion had only one commandment: "Thou shalt only dig dirt once." Our problem was that with 43 diggers, we had been potholing where we found bones, leaving piles of dirt on top of productive horizons. Then we would have to shovel those piles to get back down to the bone layers. As much as I love twice-cooked pork, the twice-dug dirt was killing us. We needed to work smarter and faster. I took to yelling, "DIG FASTER!" at the top of my lungs, in a cheery, inspirational sort of way. Actually, I was getting a little worried.

In our conversations with the reservoir project engineers, we noticed

Left: Mark Hunter confronts mud season head on. *Right:* This giant boulder came from the glacial moraine that surrounds and underlies Ziegler Reservoir.

that they had not really come to grips with the existence of the debris flows. We knew a lot about the debris flows since we were mining them by hand for their rich lode of bones. We started to realize that the engineers thought that the debris flows were actually the top of the moraine itself. We knew that they were wrong, and this meant that they were underestimating the amount of dirt that we would need to move to clear the dam face by July 1. Now we had two problems. We were digging slower that they wanted us to, and there was more dirt than they had counted on. Our problem was actually even worse than they thought it was.

We set up our surveyor's tripod and started sighting in the debris flows, and eventually we began to convince the engineers that we were nowhere near the bottom of the lake. The boulders in the debris flows, while often as big as pumpkins, were nothing like the monster boulders that the Hudick guys were finding as they were excavating near the pump house, from the actual moraine. They would occasionally drive by with a single boulder completely filling the bucket of a large loader. The debris flows really were distinct from the moraine.

And it wasn't as if the weather was cooperating. Tuesday saw an amazing transition from sun to heavy snow to hail to rain to snow to sun. It was too hot for rain gear, then too cold for the interns. I found two of them huddled and shivering in the tool trailer and sent them back to the condos for hot showers.

In the middle of this, we started our Scientists-In-Action broadcasts. Using a savvy tech team, a satellite dish, a satellite over the Galapagos Islands, and an aggressive school programs department, the museum had developed the technology and pedagogy to deliver two-way broadcasts from scientists in the field to classrooms around the country. Not only can the scien-

Just had to evacuate the site for lightning. The storm has passed and we're back at work. Was T-shirt weather but now hats and sweaters. #iceagedig
23 May

tist talk to the students, but the students can talk to the scientist. Gianna and her crew had dealt with the mercurial weather by setting up their gear in the back of a big Suburban and simply brushing the snow off the satellite dish. Then they ran a long cable down the muddy slope to cameraman Dave Baysinger, who would film one of us scientists in the muddy hole. We would wear a remote microphone and a receiver so we could speak with and hear the students. In the Suburban, Gianna's team could switch the audio from one classroom to the next.

The broadcasts would start with a brief introduction. Why was I standing in the mud and snow in the Colorado Rockies? What were all these people doing with shovels? What were we finding? Then the broadcast would switch to the students asking us questions.

We did a series of four one-hour broadcasts. It was snowing heavily, but we were finding fossils at an incredible rate and on camera. I would be talking to the students and notice that someone in the hole had just found a bone. I could then climb down into the hole and talk to that

Left: Gianna Sullivan coordinating the broadcast from the back of a suburban. *Right:* Using a satellite dish, we were able to broadcast live from the snowy dig site to classrooms around the country.

person and show the students the fossil. They were literally watching discovery happen. Joe, Ian, and I did broadcasts that morning that reached 1,200 students in 25 schools in 10 states. The crappy weather made the

broadcasts all the more exciting. At one point while I was broadcasting, Joe was walking back from the trailer with two 50-pound sacks of plaster over his shoulder. I could see him over the top of the cameraman and then he vanished! In an instant he had sunk up to his mid-thigh in the sticky mud. I started laughing, and the cameraman swung around to catch a completely mired Joe for the viewing pleasure of hundreds of students. I could hear them cracking up in their classrooms. This was even better than finding fossil bones. Scientists in action, indeed!

We had now dug to the bottom of the silt that lay below the debris flow and we discovered that the 3-foot-thick silt layer lay on top of a layer of big boulders, some as large as big pumpkins. We were delighted to discover that the boulder layer was covered in large mastodon and bison bones. The hole that Joe was digging now yielded its third mastodon pelvis.

Our media team had organized two media tours of the site, the first on

May 25 and the second on June 15. By May 25, we had laid out a trail of pallets so that it was more or less possible to walk from the Clay Mammoth to Snowy's grave, then down into the pit, and finally back up to the dam crest without being mired in sticky mud. Joe Enzer was really nervous that one of the reporters would slip and fall, but they held their footing and made it down to Joe's pelvis pit, where an entire array of large bones was exposed. In the fall, the media story had been the discovery of the mammoth in the tent. Now, the story was mastodon bones in debris flows.

On Thursday, Intern #9, Gussie Maccracken, arrived and filled out the intern corps. Gussie had just graduated from Colorado College and needed to walk across the stage before coming to Snowmass. She had worked with Ian in Wyoming the previous summer and proved to be a very solid digger. She, too, was freckled, and had a Mona Lisa smile. We didn't know it yet, but she would become the plaster intern, one of our most critical team players.

Our bone count grew to 300, and Intern #8, Nate, found a crushed bird's egg. Nate had been showing an uncanny knack for finding tiny bones. The other interns had been giving him grief for shoveling slowly, but he was actually taking time to inspect what was on his shovel blade, and that approach was paying off with a growing collection of little animal bones. Still, a fossil as delicate as a bird's egg was a completely unexpected discovery in a site that was full of rocks, logs, and bones.

Artist Jan Vriesen arrived to work on the site paintings, and he and I and several of the team geologists climbed up the Rim Trail to a vantage point where we could look down on the excavation site and up the Snowmass Creek Valley in the same field of view. From this perspective, we could see all of the landforms that made the formation of the lake basin make sense.

On Friday, we plastered the big tusk from the First Blood trench. The tusk was huge, almost 8 feet long with a big arching twist in the middle. Heather called it the monster twisty tusk. Although Heather is a skilled preparator, her team had a hard time applying the plaster jacket because the tusk, which lay at the bottom of the silt on the boulder layer, was wedged in between rocks. Even though we had found the tusk the previous Saturday, it was still in the ground. I started to think that our ability to plaster and remove the big specimens might be the key factor that would prevent us from hitting our target date. The jacket around the twisty tusk was a big, sprawling affair, and the rocks jutting up below it made the situation look pretty dodgy for "the flip." The flip is the moment in the recovery of the fossil that is the scariest for fossil diggers. Here's how they do it. First, they dig around the fossil so that it sits on a pedestal. Second, they apply a cap of plaster and burlap, sometimes adding boards or logs for strength. Third, they make an undercut below the fossil so the plaster cap is gripping the underside of the fossil, and so the fossil will stay in the jacket when the jacket is flipped. Fourth, they shave away at the pedestal until it is thin and weak. Finally, they roll (or flip) the jacket. The flip is the moment of truth.

The twisty tusk probably weighed 150 pounds. The wet sediment around it probably weighed another 100 pounds. The plaster probably weighed 100 pounds. There were a couple of two-by-fours plastered into the jacket as well. So this thing weighed upwards of 350 pounds. We gathered to watch the flip. Five big guys lined up and on the count of three began to heave the massive jacket over. The tusk was C-shaped, so as the jacket rolled, the upper part of the tusk pointed straight up with the

Finding this crushed bird's egg was astonishing.

The DMNS media team: Charlotte Hurley, Heather Hope, and Rhiannon Hendrickson.

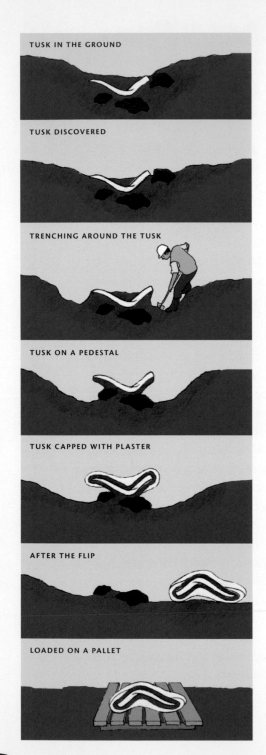

TUSK IN THE GROUND

TUSK DISCOVERED

TRENCHING AROUND THE TUSK

TUSK ON A PEDESTAL

TUSK CAPPED WITH PLASTER

AFTER THE FLIP

LOADED ON A PALLET

lower part flush to the ground. The team heaved. Then, in slow motion, the jacket came apart, the beautiful tusk broke into three even pieces, and the assembled crowd slowly realized that they should groan. After giving the flippers a few awkward looks of sympathy, everyone quietly wandered off.

Later that night, Joe, Ian, and I decided that we needed to hire someone who would do nothing but make plaster jackets. We couldn't let the jacket-making slow us down. We needed to be able to make and extract jackets in a single day. We tossed around some names and called some folks. Then Joe remembered Josh Smith, an emotive, compact Cajun paleontologist with a passion for SpongeBob SquarePants. Joe recalled that Josh was a plastering machine. When I called Josh to offer him a job, he was in Grand Junction and between jobs. He said he could be there in 24 hours. We were on our way to solving our plaster problem.

On Saturday, after working 14 straight days, we decided to give the crew a day off. Everybody, that is, except for Joe and Carlos. They spent the day running the mini-excavator and cleaning up the site.

Week Three: Mud Season Ends
SUNDAY, MAY 29–SATURDAY, JUNE 4, 2011

Finally the weather seemed to be changing. It was sunny and windy, and amazingly, it was a bit dusty. Our third team had arrived, and we oriented them to the safety and story of the site and started them digging. Josh arrived and recruited some volunteers to create the Plaster Team, or Team P, as it came to be known. This was our 16th day on the site, and I was starting to wonder why we had not found bones of any large carnivore.

Every fossil site has its own story, and I pondered what kind of story would yield a bucolic world with no predators.

Top: Volunteer Alex Prinster digs around the edge of a big mastodon pelvis. *Bottom:* Intern Tyler Kerr has a Flintstone moment.

In the fall, I was content to think that our sample size wasn't large enough and that with more bones, we would eventually get our predator. But now we were getting more bones but still no predator.

This made me start thinking about other famous sites with large ice age mammals and their stories. The big daddy of them all is the La Brea tar seeps in downtown Los Angeles, which were formed when natural petroleum seeped from underground reservoirs to the surface and evaporated from liquid to super sticky asphalt. An animal like a bison that walked through one of these water-covered seeps could easily get stuck, and a bison that can't move is also known as hamburger. Passing carnivores couldn't resist a free burger, so they hopped on for a free lunch and found themselves stuck as well. In this way, even predators like saber-toothed cats, dire wolves, American lions, and short-faced bears became hamburgers themselves. For this reason, La Brea is known as a predator trap, with more than 75 percent of the bones found there coming from predators.

There are other kinds of traps as well. Among my favorites are the pitfall traps. The best one is a site near Lovell, Wyoming, named Natural Trap—a cave shaped like a bottle with a 20-foot opening at the top and an 80-foot depth. Each year, snow drifted across the top of the cave and concealed its dangers. Unlucky animals wandering across the landscape in the late spring dropped through the rotten snow, falling 80 feet to their death. This natural trap has been open for business for at least the last 100,000 years, and its floor is covered in a pyramid of bones and skeletons of both predators and herbivores.

The Mammoth Site at Hot Springs, South Dakota, is yet another type of trap. It is the remains of a sinkhole lake that formed when the limestone roof of a cave collapsed under the weight of a thick overlying layer of clay. The result was an enticing lake with slick clay walls. Animals that were lured by the siren's song of a long cool drink found that they couldn't escape and they couldn't tread water forever. This natural trap mainly contained mammoths—something like 55 Columbian mammoths and three woolly mammoths—but it has also produced a short-faced bear, one of the more fearsome ice age predators. Who knows if he was attracted by the bloated carcasses of mammoths, or if he too was in search of some cool water.

Plenty of fossil sites were not traps at all but simply places where animals died over time and their bones accumulated. A great example of one of these sites is Bonney Springs, Missouri, which has produced more than 700 bones,

Joe Sertich hoists a massive mastodon femur.

representing parts of 31 mastodons. Bonney Springs appears to be a place where animals came to drink and where they came to die. It was more like a hospice than a death trap. Bonney Springs also holds the world's record for the most mastodons in a single site, and I was starting to wonder if Snowmass was going to give Bonney Springs a run for its money.

We still couldn't tell if Glacial Lake Ziegler was a trap or a hospice. If it was a trap, we had no idea of the trapping mechanism. And we had utterly no clue why we weren't finding predators. By the beginning of week three, speculation was rampant among the diggers—it seemed like everyone was inventing their own theory for why Lake Ziegler was full of bones.

I was thinking about other things, specifically how I was going to pay for this massive effort. While meeting with people in Aspen over the spring, several had suggested that we charge donors for the right to visit the site. That seemed like a pretty mercenary way to go, and we had backed off. Some potential donors we brought to the site were kind enough to write a check to the project. The previous week, I had impressed a visitor by claiming I could find a bone in five minutes and then proceeded to uncover one in four.

On Sunday, May 29, Iris Smith, two of her adult children, and one of their friends visited the site. Iris was in town from California, and one of our friends thought that she might be willing to support our effort. Right off the bat she offered me $5,000 if I could find her a bone in less than 10 minutes. Ian and I sharpened our shovels and went to work. Four minutes later a mastodon rib popped out of the ground and we won the reward. I don't know what got into me, but somehow I thought Iris might be game. I winked at her and said, "Double or nothing?" She didn't pause for a second and answered, "You bet." Wondering if it was legal to gamble with museum assets, I started digging like a mad badger. Forty-four seconds later, a lovely bison maxilla complete with three shiny teeth made me an honest man.

On Monday, the weather switched back to snow and our bone count climbed to 546. A bunch of our scientist team had chosen this week for their big field effort, and more than two dozen of them showed up to begin collecting samples and deciphering the site. Nat Lifton from Purdue was here to sample the boulders in the moraine, using a method called

Iris Smith and the $10,000 bison maxilla.

cosmogenic dating that measures how long the boulder had been exposed to sunlight and cosmic rays. This would give us a minimum date for the age of the moraine—a number that we suspected would be around 130,000 years. Shannon Mahan from the U.S. Geological Survey, was doing the same thing in reverse. She was using metal cylinders to sample the lake sediment to measure how long it had been since the silt grains had seen the sun. Her method is called optically stimulated luminescence, or OSL for short. Jeff Pigati led a large group of geologists who measured the thickness of each layer of lake-filling sediment and explored and mapped the moraine. We were well on our way to figuring this thing out.

On Tuesday the engineers informed us that we had now moved 750 yards. We had been digging for 15 days and were averaging 50 yards a day. That was better, but we probably needed to be doing about 85 yards a day to move 4,000 yards by July 1. We still weren't digging fast enough. I knew we could fit more diggers on the site, and I started thinking about people I knew who were experienced shovelers. Over the years, a lot of interns, students, and friends have come to the field with me. I figured that we could easily add a dozen diggers without straining the supply system too badly. With only a month to go before the deadline, I was not interested in getting to July 1 with a big pile of unexplored dirt

in front of me. I decided to see if we could sprint for two weeks, aiming to substantially finish the dig by June 17 rather than July 1, and use the last two weeks as a careful wrap-up.

As a paleobotanist, I come from a background that prizes pickaxes, shovels, and digging, and am proud to be called a leaf digger. One of my battle cries is "You can't find a big fossil leaf on a small rock." Over the past 30 years, I had created a cult of diggers who enjoyed the moving of rock and the creation of big quarries almost as much as the finding of fossils. So I made phone calls to a few dozen hardened diggers from my past who lived in Chicago, New York, Grand Junction, Seattle, North Dakota, Boston, Denver, and Salt Lake City. About half of them dropped what they were doing and headed for Snowmass. For the first time, I could see how we might reach our goal.

Bones started flying out of the ground. May 30 was the first day that we found more than 100 bones in a single day. I found a completely amazing mastodon mandible. It was still white and hardly looked like it was old. The jaw had a splendid pair of mandibular tusks, little club-like tusks that protruded from the end of the animal's chin. I'd never even heard of chin tusks. Krista spent most of her days in the con-

dominiums organizing daily logistics. On this day, she and her fiancé, Kit, were digging side by side when he found a stunning tusk. It, too, was unstained and looked like it had just fallen off a living mastodon. It started snowing again, but there were so many bones that I didn't even pay attention. Intern #4, Tyler, was digging with me, and we found a black, shiny object with really distinctive bands. It looked like an ancient marine animal called a trilobite, but it turned out to be a huge, magnificent mastodon tooth. I was having the time of my life.

Left: Cayce Gulbransen pounds steel tubes into the sedimentary layers exposed at the big wall. This is the first step in taking suitable samples for optically stimulated luminescence (OSL) dating. The yellow layer near the base of the wall later yielded a date of about 100,000 years. *Right:* Kevin Burr, the foreman for Hudick Excavating Inc., with an adult mastodon tooth.

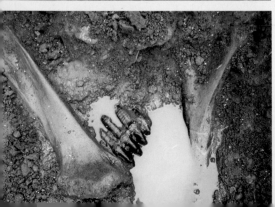

May 31 felt like the first day of summer, sunny and warm. One of our volunteers, Becky Shorey, found the skull of a baby mastodon. That seemed odd. Fossils of babies are rare. Maybe it was a clue. The presence of babies seemed to support the idea of a trap. We wondered if landslides or avalanches were the cause of mastodon death, but that didn't make sense because we were finding isolated bones rather than whole skeletons. We were definitely missing something and it was frustrating not to be able to answer the obvious question: Why were these bones here?

I wondered out loud, half joking, if the trapping mechanism was like a huge ant lion trap. Ant lions are predatory insect larvae that bury themselves at the bottom of conical holes in dry sand. While the hole may only be an inch deep, it is the perfect size, roundness, and steepness that a wandering ant that falls in the hole is unable to escape. It's hard to believe it until you see an ant frantically trying to scramble up the tiny slope, unable to make any progress. If the ant gets near the top, then the ant lion flicks a spray of sand and knocks it back down. Then comes the amazing moment when the jaws of the ant lion rise out of the bottom of the hole and grab the hapless ant, pulling it under. These things are scarier than the sand worms from the novel *Dune.* I imagined a moraine slope full of round boulders, the perfect size so that mastodons could get in but not out. It was a fun idea, but not a very good one, and it didn't explain why we had bones and not skeletons. Not all ideas are worth prolonged thought.

We had used one of the large track hoes to dig a series of long trenches down the hill to expose the sedimentary layers so that we could measure and understand them. We also dug a bunch of deep holes around the margin of the lake to see if bones extended beyond the reach of our excavation. They did. At one point, the bucket pulled up some big logs from one of the trenches on the north side of the dam face. The logs didn't strike me as unusual at first, since we had routinely seen wood in the debris flows. A pair of big vertebrae was under one of the logs, and I set Brendan Asher, an archaeologist, to the task of exposing the bones, because archaeologists have way more patience than paleontologists. The next day, I wandered back to where Brendon was still working with a team of three others. They had exhumed an ancient shoreline complete with driftwood. The logs continued along the hillside and were clearly worthy of further investigation. I told him to keep digging to see what he could find.

Top: Oh the joy! My first mastodon mandible. *Middle:* Kit and his perfect little tusk. *Bottom:* Mastodon bones and a perfect, shiny black tooth. *Right:* Ant lion pit in Utah.

The mystery of the many bones was really starting to bug me. The bones we were finding down in the hole were mainly mastodon, with a smattering of bison and sloth. On June 2, URS sent their crack geologist, Dale Baures, to the site, and I walked around with him. He agreed with our assessment that the bone/boulder/log-rich layers were debris flows. By now we had realized that there were more than one of these, and they all had bones. Whatever had happened to kill and bury mastodons at this lake had happened more than once. Dale cracked me up when he called the site a "mastodon coquina." A coquina is a geologic term usually used to describe geologic layers that are made almost entirely of little shells.

The third week ended strongly, with our bone count at 955. Russ Forrest, the Snowmass Village town manager, invited the entire crew to his house for a cookout, and about 45 of us showed up at his door. Our caterer had been bombarding us with chicken for a couple of weeks, so we were all ravenously seeking red meat. The cookout was in Russ's backyard,

Left: Nat Lifton on the moraine with a soil pit and a large boulder that he will date with the cosmogenic technique. *Right:* These ancient driftwood logs were aligned parallel to the edge of the lake. We had found a beach.

but when the sun went down, the temperature dropped rapidly. Soon we were jammed in his living room munching on burgers.

June 4 was a sunny, hazy day, and for the first time in 22 days, we didn't send a single digger to the site. Everybody needed a rest. I drove down to Carbondale for lunch with Jim Calaway to seek fund-raising advice. As I was sitting with him at the restaurant, I realized that I had forgotten my wallet. That was not a good start, but he had a good laugh at my expense and generously bought me lunch.

On the way back upvalley I stopped in El Jebel to find Vaughn Shafer. Snowmass Mayor Bill Boineau had told me about Vaughn, a local blacksmith who had a deep interest in ice age animals. He was the creator of the El Jebel town sign, a double-sized steel elk skull. I didn't have an address, so I just drove around town looking for a blacksmith shop. With an eye for forged steel, it didn't take long for me to find a likely shop. I parked my truck and pounded on the door. After a few seconds, Vaughn opened the door and welcomed me warmly. Wearing an orange Sturgis vest and a blue skull-and-crossbones do-rag, he looked a lot more like a biker than a blacksmith. It turns out that he was both, a third-generation blacksmith

by trade and a biker and stuntman by preference. He offered me a Bud Light, which I accepted, and we pulled up chairs. My eyes immediately lit on a big ol' Harley that was fabricated with forged steel to form the quite accurate and somewhat intimidating skeleton of a full-sized saber-toothed cat. This guy was the real deal.

Vaughn couldn't have been more pleased with my visit. He showed me around his workshop and told me how he had proposed to build full-sized steel skeletons of all the Snowmass animals for the town. He had already presented a proposal to Russ Forrest and Bill Boineau. The more I saw, the more I thought that this might be a viable idea. One of the interesting by-products of all the multimillion-dollar homes in the Roaring Fork Valley is the presence of amazing craftspeople. Vaughn took me to the next shop over and introduced me to Samuel Gonzalez de la Rosa, a master wood-carver, who was putting the finishing touches on a stunning bear carving.

My truck was full of Snowmass bones, so I unpacked a big mastodon rib to show to the two craftsmen. They were amazed that I had brought show-and-tell, and I was pumped to see how excited they were. Here were guys who fabricated amazing things all day long, and I was able to show them something that blew their minds. We talked about the dig for more than an hour before I had to leave. I would be back.

Below: Samuel Gonzalez de la Rosa and Vaughn Shafer enjoy a mastodon rib. *Right:* Blacksmith Vaughn Shafer transformed a Harley hog into an ice age saber-toothed cat.

Mud season was over and summer had truly begun, evidenced by the fact that Snowmass was staging its Chili Pepper and Brew Fest. Hundreds of people poured into town to drink beer, eat chili, and listen to some rock and roll. I had promised Susan Hamley from Snowmass Tourism that I would show up on stage that Saturday night and talk about the dig. I stopped at the condos, collected Ian and Joe, and grabbed the big rib that had just impressed the blacksmith.

The band that night was the Tedeschi Trucks Band. Ian, Joe, and I went on stage before the band came out and we delivered a brief lecture about mastodons, which basically consisted of me yelling, "Snowmass Rocks and Mastodons Rule! Change the name of Snowmass to Snowmastodon." When we climbed off the stage, there were Susan Tedeschi and Derek Trucks. We posed for a picture with them, and I nearly thwacked Derek in the nose with the mastodon rib. Ian turned to Susan and whispered, "Do you want to dig with us?" Susan replied, "Hell, yeah!"

Week Four: Teacher Diggers
SUNDAY, JUNE 5—SATURDAY, JUNE 11, 2011

The next morning I pulled up in front of the Silvertree Hotel at 7 a.m. sharp, not at all sure that there would be anybody there to pick up. But, true to their word, Derek and Susan strolled out of the hotel, hopped in the truck, and we drove to the site. Joe, Ian, and Ian's wife, Robyn, were already there. I was surprised to see Robyn, an urban hipster floral designer, who had previously sworn that she would never go digging with us. Suddenly she was a fossil digger.

Susan Tedeschi turned out to be a really good digger. The band only had an hour before they had to rush back to catch a flight out of Aspen and she dove right in, shoveling like a pro. After about 20 minutes, she struck bone, a big one. It took another 20 minutes with three of us bamboo-ing away to free the perfect mastodon ulna from its rocky grave. It was full of mastodon juice, of which we all imbibed. I drove them back to their world of rock and roll and returned to my world of rocks and bones.

Our first group of Roaring Fork teachers reported for work on June 4. They joined a rapidly growing shovel corps that allowed us to put more than 50 people on the ground at a time. Kit arranged for us to rent a couple of skid steers, small vehicles with big 1-cubic-yard buckets that would let us start moving dirt away from our digs. We started to crank.

I continued wandering around the site yelling, "DIG FASTER!" And then, realizing that I didn't just want people to dig faster but also wanted them to find cool stuff, I would yell, "BRING ME THE HEAD OF ZIGGY THE SLOTH!"

Left: Kirk and Snowy backstage. *Top right:* Joe, Derek Trucks, Kirk, a mastodon rib, Ian, and Susan Tedeschi just before the Tedeschi Trucks Band concert, Snowmastodon Rocks! *Bottom right:* Susan Tedeschi, a fabulous musician and a fine digger to boot, with Ian's wife, Robyn.

By June 6, the bone count stood at 1,292. While we were digging big bones, Richard Stucky led a team down at Snowmass Water and Sanitation that was washing dirt through screens in an attempt to find tiny bones. He was supported by Dena Meade-Hunter, a museum volunteer who has been working with me since 1993. Richard and Dena traded off the role of screen-washing captain and piled up many tiny bones, mainly salamander. It will take us a long time to get an accurate count on the small bones at the site. In addition to screening sediment on site, we were also collecting bags of sediment to be taken to Denver to be washed and sorted in the future.

At the weekly construction meeting on Tuesday, Dave Lady from URS had good news and bad news for us. By his calculation, we had moved 1,000 yards of dirt by shovel! Then he told us that his calculations had also moved the target amount to be moved from 4,000 to 6,000 yards. I glanced over at Ian and he nodded. The goalposts had just been moved by 50 yards. We were beginning to wonder what they were measuring. In any case, we could see the dirt that needed to be moved fast. Ian, Joe, and I were constantly strategizing how we could move it faster. Joe Enzer was a huge help, always sauntering up with little suggestions of how we could up our productivity. Kit also started sending other equipment and staff to help

Carlos out. We learned how to operate the skid steers and started moving dirt ourselves. We started paying Carlos overtime to keep him after hours and on weekends. The engineers and the Snowmass Water and Sanitation District were measuring our progress by how much dirt we moved. Our measure of success was the bone count.

June 7 was a big day for bones. We found more than 200 bones in a single day for the first time. More digging, more bones. We found three perfect sloth claws, a *Megalonyx* hat trick. That afternoon, as we were wrapping up for the day, a huge black bear wandered onto the edge of the excavation. Clearly interested in us or our lunches, he sauntered into the woods about 200 yards away, settling down to watch us. We took this as a sign that it was time to go to dinner. The more optimistic of us took it as a sign that we would soon find our carnivore.

The next day, I drove into Aspen to record a television piece with Jerry Bovino. Jerry is a fast-talking East Coast guy who somehow washed up in Aspen doing community TV. He had prepared for our conversation, and we had a blast with the banter. Jerry called the episode, "Fossil Boy." I liked

Top right: Bethany Williams using running water and a gentle brush to clean dirt from a mastodon bone. *Left:* Kirk yelling to inspire the diggers to dig faster.

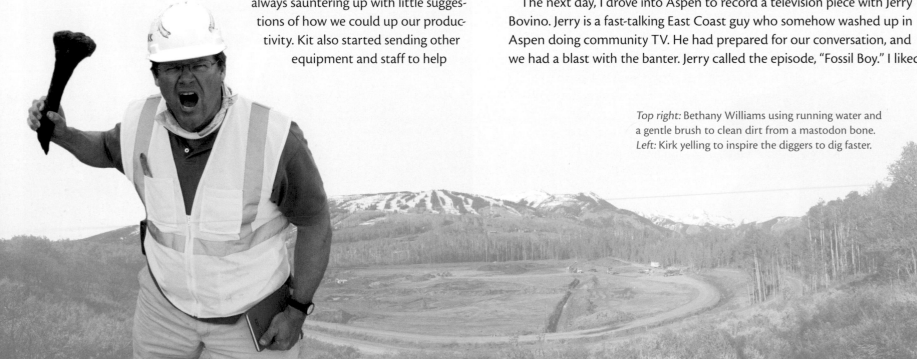

that moniker, so I wrote it on my hard hat. Then I stopped by the Aspen Historical Society to give them a report on the dig. The place was quiet, but I eventually found staff member Nina Gabianelli, who had just arrived with a freshly baked rhubarb pie. I traded a private viewing of one of the sloth claws for a slice of pie. I remembered a sign from Hannibal, Missouri: "Here stood the board fence which Tom Sawyer persuaded his gang to pay him for the privilege of whitewashing. Tom sat by and saw that it was done well." I enjoyed the pie.

Back on site, I ran into James Simon, the main equipment operator for Hudick Excavating Inc. Earlier in the week, I had learned that he had been a dozer operator at a housing development in Brighton, Colorado, back in 2003, when a museum volunteer discovered a beautiful *Triceratops* skull. I had challenged the museum volunteers to find a *Triceratops* for the museum in this metro-area construction site, and one of them had

Left: By sifting the sediment and carefully searching for tiny bones, we were able to find evidence of a surprisingly diverse group of small animals including cutthroat trout, tiger salamanders, frogs, garter snakes, rattlesnakes, lizards, ducks, geese, grouse, finches, shore birds, shrews, weasels, otters, beavers, red-backed voles, bog lemmings, muskrats, deer mice, harvest mice, chipmunks, golden-mantled ground squirrels, kangaroo rats, pocket gophers, jumping mice, rabbits, and pikas.

Bottom left: Paula Meadows and a near perfect claw of *Megalonyx jeffersonii*.
Right: On June 7, this big, black bear visited the site. Too bad we never found his fossil cousins.

Gussie Mccracken,
the queen of Team P.

actually done it. James, it turns out, is one of those operators who pays attention to what he moves. He and Kevin Burr, his foreman, had been a bit reserved at the beginning of the dig, but soon they, too, were drawn into the excitement. When James saw my hard hat with its new "Fossil Boy" inscription, he couldn't help but laugh. He couldn't believe that a big man would allow himself to be called a boy. Not a problem: I had a lot of fence to white wash.

The No Bone Left Behind Challenge was heating up. Dane's Team Trench was ahead with 427 bones. Heather's Team Tiger Salamander was barely holding on to second place with 353 bones. Bryan's Team Mammoth was closing on Heather with 347 bones. Joe's Team Sloth was pulling up the rear with 332 bones. By Friday, June 10, we had moved 1,800 yards of dirt and found

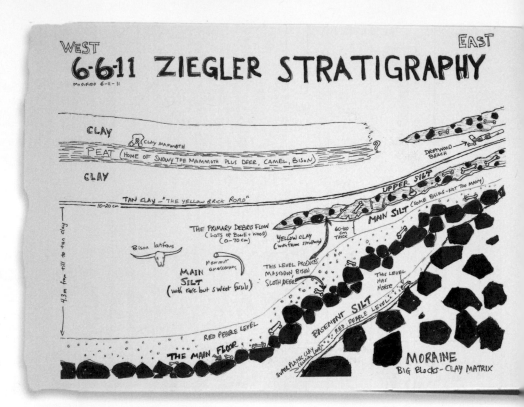

This diagram that I drew on June 6 shows how well we understood the layers of fossil-bearing sediment.

ICE AGE CAMEL
Camelops sp.

ICE AGE HORSE
Equus sp.

MULE DEER
Odocoileus sp.

GIANT ICE AGE BISON
Bison latifrons

JEFFERSON'S GROUND SLOTH
Megalonyx jeffersonii

Cherrie Catlin was mesmerized by the dig. She spent days watching discoveries being made.

more than 250 bones in a single day for the first time.

Joe, Carlos, Alice Steindler (one of the Roaring Fork teacher-diggers from Rifle High School), and the entire Miller family decided to work on June 11, an official day off. It was a gorgeous, sunny day, and I tried to spend it hanging out by the pool at the Snowmass Club. The problem is that I'm not really a pool guy, so after a while, I headed back to the site. The small group was having a banner day and had found more than 60 bones by themselves. Carlos had managed to dig a trench all the way to the bottom of the lake and exposed the top of the moraine for the first time. This allowed us to see the bottom of the lake and clearly understand just how much work was in front of us.

Based on what we learned that day, I drew the first accurate diagram of the sediment layers that had filled the glacial lake. This drawing was the road map that we would use to complete the dig. We named the layers and would use those names to communicate with the diggers. The boulder floor that produced all the pelvises back in May was actually not the moraine but a rocky layer about 3 feet above it that we called the Main Floor. When Carlos punched through the Main Floor he found another layer of silt below it, which we called the Basement Silt. Joe crawled down into the Basement Silt and discovered parts of a big elephant (we weren't sure if it was a mammoth or mastodon) and the distinctive leg bone of an ice age horse. The Snowmass fauna now included seven large mammals.

Alice Steindler, a teacher-digger from Rifle High School excavates a bison skull.

AMERICAN MASTODON
Mammut americanum

COLUMBIAN MAMMOTH
Mammuthus columbi

Week Five: The Head of Ziggy the Sloth
SUNDAY, JUNE 12–SATURDAY, JUNE 18, 2011

By June 12, we were digging at an amazing pace. A new team of volunteers arrived, and was swiftly oriented. A new batch of Roaring Fork teachers arrived, and some from the previous week refused to leave because they were having too much fun.

On this perfect Colorado day we were having what my artist friend Guy Anderson once called "Agooddiggingday." I spent much of the afternoon with a family of museum supporters, the Thompsons. Jack and Viki Thompson had a house in Snowmass and they were building a bigger one. When in Denver, they would often drop by the museum with their sweet little granddaughters, Chloe and Quinn. Over the last year, I had grown quite fond of the girls and was happy to see them on the site. They were too young to dig, so I spent much of the afternoon playing with them and throwing mud clods in a trench full of water. The rest of the family, which included some teenaged boys and their parents, was digging in a layer just above the Main Floor that we called the Red Pebble Layer. They dug patiently for a couple of hours, excited at the prospect of finding fossils. They found a few scraps of bone, but nothing of note. It was too bad. I hate it when people get skunked. They left, happy to have been there, but without a life-transforming discovery.

I wandered back to where they had been digging and started slowly shoveling. It was getting late in the afternoon. I didn't expect to find anything, but sometimes I relax by shoveling.

As I was quietly digging, winding down from playing with the girls, the tip of my shovel grazed the tip of something hard. On the follow-through, I flicked off a slice of silt, exposing the perfect gleaming tip of a large mastodon tusk. Life is good. I dropped to my knees and pulled out my bamboo tool. It really was the tip, and it was really big. Forty-five minutes later, I exposed an 8-foot-long and essentially perfect tusk. Agooddiggingday indeed.

The rest of the diggers worked hard and fast, but I figured that a little motivation couldn't hurt. I was regularly yelling, "DIG FASTER AND BRING ME THE HEAD OF ZIGGY THE SLOTH!" Yelling was good, but

It must be the end of a long day since six people are watching while only two are digging.

then I realized, why not offer a bounty? At the recap after dinner that night, I promised a GPS device and a bottle of Stranahan's Whiskey to the person who brought me the head of Ziggy the sloth.

On June 13, at 10:49 a.m., I got a call from Peter Ziegler. His sister Cherrie told him that I was now offering a bounty for the discovery of a sloth skull. He wanted to let me now that he was coming to join the dig with his wife, Joan, and four of their Wisconsin friends. He also wanted to throw $100 into the pool for whoever found the sloth skull.

I spent the rest of the morning with Kirk Johnson, the Denver bureau chief for *The New York Times*. Since he and I shared a name, we had known about each other for nearly a decade but, we had only met the previous fall when we were booked back-to-back as lecturers in a class at the University of Colorado at Boulder. Kirk often writes about environmental issues in the American West, and I was used to receiving congratulatory e-mails from my friends when one of his articles was published. For years, I hoped to make a discovery that was large enough that it couldn't be ignored by my homonym at *The New York Times*. Snowmass was that discovery. Kirk spent two hours with me and wrote a piece for the Tuesday *Science Times*, which ran on July 5. It was entitled, "Pleistocene

ACT THREE

Treasures, at a Breakneck Pace." The headline captured it all, but the coup for me was that the piece about one Kirk Johnson was written by another Kirk Johnson. Despite his explicit disclaimer, I still received dozens of e-mails congratulating me on the article that I had written for *The New York Times*.

After Kirk left, I retreated to Big Blue to take a break and savor the day. I often parked at the top of the dam. From that vantage point I could watch the entire excavation while I was taking media calls, checking e-mail, and communicating with the museum. At 2 p.m., I glanced out the window of the truck to see Joe Sertich sprinting up the hill. My first thought was "Who's hurt?" I opened the door just as Joe reached the top of the hill and blurted out, "Chris Faison found Ziggy's head."

I ran down the hill to a small mound just above the Main Floor, where Chris Faison, a teacher-digger, was surrounded by the entire digging crew. The crowd parted to let me pass. There, still in the ground, was an unmistakably perfect skull of *Megalonyx jeffersonii*, Jefferson's ground sloth, Ziggy. I wanted to cry. I did cry. I never thought that we would actually find Ziggy's head; I just wanted to make sure that people had something to dig for.

Chris Faison was sitting down, but he was also floating a few feet above the ground. I was stunned. Chris was the guy who had built the giant cardboard mammoth in his classroom at Aspen Community School. Ziggy's head couldn't have been found by a better person. The discovery belonged to the Roaring Fork Valley. I told Chris about Peter's recent phone call. Chris told me that by all means he would accept the Stranahan's Whiskey, but he thought I ought to give the GPS and the $100 to the interns (I was so happy that I ended up giving them $100 each).

The skull was firmly wedged between the boulders of the Main Floor. The extraction was going to be tricky, and it would require a plaster jacket. Chris spent the rest of the afternoon carefully removing the treasure. I went back to the truck and called Peter Ziegler: "You're not going to believe this, but …"

Around midday, my artist friends Ray Troll and Gary Staab showed up at the site. Ray was already invested in the site, having written the Snowmastodon song. He and I have been traveling a lot together, researching a

Left: A very happy Chris Faison and the plastered skull of Ziggy the sloth. *Right:* The nearly complete and much awaited skull of Ziggy the sloth.

book project about the fossils of the Pacific Coast. We had spent a week the previous June at the La Brea Tar Pits in Los Angeles, so we were already deeply seeped in conversations about ice age animals. It occurred to me that Snowmastodon could be Colorado's La Brea.

Gary used to work at the museum before going freelance. He builds life-sized sculptures of prehistoric beasts. Some of his sculptures are massive. He had recently won a public art contest and installed a life-size long-neck dinosaur sculpture in an elevator courtyard of the museum's new underground parking garage. Both Ray and Gary had worked to develop the *Amazon Voyage* exhibit, and I wanted to make sure they had firsthand experiences in Snowmass. You just never know what might result.

Left: Ray Troll and a sample of what he will do if given hard hats and Sharpies. *Right:* I wore my promises on my head: $500 bounty for *Arctodus*, the giant short-faced bear. Sadly, I did not have to pay.

In any case, it's always good to have artists on site. I equipped them with shovels and bamboo and showed them how to dig. Ray is a notoriously unlucky fossil finder, but even he was soon pulling out bones.

At the end of the day, I carried the 40-pound plaster block that contained Ziggy's head to Big Blue and drove it back to the condo, where I placed it on the center of the coffee table. I wasn't ready for it to leave my sight.

June 14 was the biggest bone day yet. We found more than 300 bones, breaking our single-day record and driving the bone count to 2,832. We had moved 2,700 yards of dirt. The plan was working, but I needed a new incentive now that Ziggy was in the bag. I took a Sharpie and wrote "$500 for *Arctodus*" on my hard hat. We still hadn't found our carnivore, and what could be better than the skull of *Arctodus*, the giant short-faced bear?

When it comes to writing on hard hats, I am a rank amateur compared to Ray. Ray has a wild pen, and he will draw on anything that doesn't move. Many of the diggers were Troll fans, and I noticed that hard hats were getting Trollified.

Ray is also a bit of a choreographer, and he saw what I had been missing. We had become a tribe of shovel people. The Impis of Zulu warriors had nothing on us. Ray organized us into a group and made us all raise our

shovels to the sky. Move the goal posts all you want—the Denver Museum of Nature & Science will dig its way to the end zone.

As the work continued and the size of the team grew, we added more team captains. We chose people who have volunteered with us for years and who demonstrated that curious mix of skills that qualifies as dig leadership. These people know how to find fossils, break rock, weather bad weather, gently wrap fragile specimens, and keep their team laughing the whole time. Steve Wagner is a young retiree from the Silicon Valley rat race who became our digital leaf guru. Jim Cornette is a retired math professor from Iowa whose memory,

energy, and humor laughs at his actual age. Fritz Koether is a cool, collected guy with a mustache that reminds me of my fondness for walrus.

I wandered over to the crew working for Jim and saw that he took his captain duties seriously. He took pains to point out the skills and background of each of his diggers. They had just uncovered a large mastodon humerus and were posing with the fossil as it lay in the ground. I stuck around and helped them loosen, then lift, the 60-pound bone. As the

Aspen teachers Georgina Levey (left) and Kristin Lidman (right), and intern Hannah O'Neill (center) work down through the main silt layer, that lies on top of the bones and stones of the Main Floor. We described these layers as we dug them, allowing us to reconstruct the sequence of events that transpired as the ancient lake filled over tens of thousands of years.

bone came free, Bob Buck, a volunteer in his mid-60s, looked at me and said, "I've been waiting since I was six years old for this moment."

By June 16, members of the museum's board started trickling in to the site. We had arranged to have our annual board retreat in Snowmass Village. It was clear to both George and me that this was probably the single most significant excavation in the museum's 111-year history, and we wanted the board to experience it firsthand.

Peter Dea, board president and a very thoughtful guy, brought me a bottle of Stranahan's Whiskey as a gift. He had no way of knowing that I owed one to Chris Faison, nor that these bottles were getting hard to find in the Roaring Fork Valley. I stuffed it in my pack and kept digging. A few minutes later, I looked up, and there was George Stranahan himself. He was with his wife, Patti, and Anita Thompson, wife of the late Hunter S. Thompson. Clearly, the best way to meet the iconic figures of the Roaring Fork Valley was to open a major excavation. Chris Faison and fellow teacher-digger Alice Steindler had invited Stranahan to see the site. I was delighted to be able to show him that I always kept a bottle of his whiskey handy. Later that night, I passed the bottle off to Chris, having used it socially three times without ever getting to sip it once.

We had planned a big weekend for the board with meetings, visits to the site, dinners, fund-raising parties for the project, and demonstrations of the museum's outreach efforts related to the dig. We had arranged for another Ice Age Spectacular festival at the Silvertree Hotel. We visited schools and libraries with our *Time Scene Investigation* show. We did a live Scientists-In-Action broadcast from the site to the festival. And most importantly, we let the board members dig. On June 18, while the board was on site, Aspen teacher Andre Wille uncovered one of the most beautiful fossils of the entire dig. He was working with Jim Cornette's crew on the very south end of the excavation, boring sideways into the vertical wall. Andre uncovered what he first thought to be a tusk. Once more dirt was removed, it was clear that it was the lower jaw of a massive male mastodon, complete with unworn and glistening black teeth and prodigious chin tusks. It looked like it was a staged event, but, in reality, it was an amazing and timely discovery.

Left: DMNS board member John Freyer, his wife, Ginny, and a mastodon ulna. *Right:* Kirk just happened to have a bottle of Stranahan's Whiskey in his rucksack when George Stranahan visited the dig. *Opposite left:* Aspen teacher Andre Wille found this magnificent mastodon mandible complete with mandibular (chin) tusks. *Opposite top right:* Jim Cornette and his team hoist yet another mastodon humerus. *Opposite bottom right:* Bamboo tools were the secret to digging bones without scratching them.

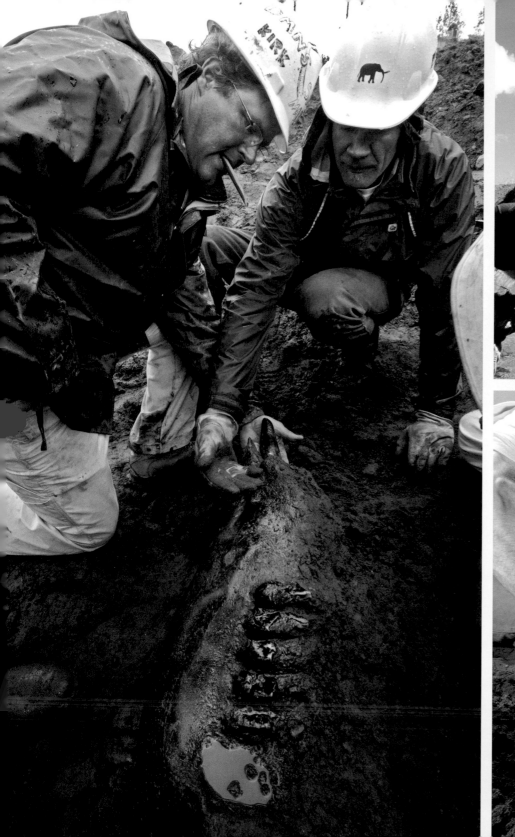

Week Six: Big Science
SUNDAY, JUNE 19–SATURDAY, JUNE 25, 2011

Week six promised to be the largest of the entire excavation. We had a new batch of Roaring Fork educators; Richard Stucky brought eight of his Teen Science Scholars; 37 scientists were scheduled to arrive; and we had a new crew of Denver and Roaring Fork volunteers. Fortunately, we had made incredible progress the previous week, and we were definitely and comfortably on our way to a successful completion by July 1.

On June 19 Dan Fisher pulled me aside and said that he had a testable hypothesis for why we had so many mastodons. He had been thinking about the earthquake-induced debris flow theory, but he had taken the idea a step further. He proposed that the animals were actually in the lake when an earthquake had occurred. The earthquake caused liquefaction of the lake bed silts, causing the animals to sink into quicksand and get stuck. Then it was just a matter of time before they starved to death and many more months before their bones would litter the lake floor. Then a subsequent earthquake would cause the debris flow that deposited their scattered bones down the underwater slope. He figured that he could test the idea by sectioning the tusks and seeing if they all showed the same season of death. If they all died at the same time, then it was a positive

test. If they died at different times, then a less catastrophic cause would be indicated.

I liked the hypothesis and the test. At least this explanation lined up with the observation that we had scattered but pristine bones. I immediately coined this hypothesis the "shake-kill-pause-shake-bury" hypothesis. The test will take months of careful work in Dan's Michigan laboratory to slice the tusks and measure the growth rings.

Over at the Clay Mammoth, Dan and his team were puzzled. Earlier in the dig, Bryan Small and his team had exposed a skull with an attached tusk, a jaw, a scapula, and some ribs of the big male mammoth. While exposing the bones, they also discovered a number of soccer-ball-sized rocks. Some were below the bones, some were above them, and some were between them. This was really odd because the partial skeleton was in the middle of the lake and it was buried in the fine clay that lay on top of the peat. There didn't seem to be a simple explanation for why large rocks were associated with the skeleton.

Dan had done a lot of previous work on mastodon kill sites in the upper Midwest, where he discovered that early human hunters would cache meat in the bottom of ponds. That solved a couple of problems for them. If a hunter was lucky enough to kill a big animal like a mastodon, he would have food for a long time,

Left: Hendrik Poinar from McMasters University samples bone for ancient DNA. *Right:* Team Tiger Salamander captain Heather Finlayson and a sweet little mastodon tusk.

but the meat would start to spoil and it would attract big scavengers and predators. The solution for both of the problems was to make a hide rope, tie rocks to the big meat shanks to weigh them down, then sink them to the bottom of an ice-covered lake. This way they could come back later and retrieve the meat. The lake would act as a meat locker. Dan even tested this idea by butchering a dead draft horse and storing it in a Michigan lake. Appallingly, he would pull up the shanks each month and cook and eat a small piece to see if the method worked. He is still with us, so it must have.

The problem with the Clay Mammoth being a meat cache was its age. Our early radiocarbon results had suggested that the clay was more than 45,000 years old. The earliest firm evidence for humans in North America is only about 13,800 years. Either our dates were wrong and it was a human meat cache, or, more likely, there was some geological explanation for the big rocks and the age was correct.

Nonetheless, even if there was a 1/10th of 1 percent chance that the site was both old and human, we needed to be extremely cautious about how we handled the specimen. After a long pow-wow, we decided to remove the entire specimen in a single huge block. Bryan and his team set about the process of building a structure to do just that.

By June 21 the bone count was up to 4,056, we had moved 4,500 yards of dirt, and Dane and Team Trench had pulled into an unbeatable lead with 1,141 bones. Joe and Team Sloth were in second place with 864 bones. Heather was in third with 778 bones, and Bryan, due to his focus on the Clay Mammoth, was falling way behind with 643 bones.

Teams of scientists swarmed over the site collecting all manner of samples. Jeff Honke from the U.S. Geological Survey arrived with a drill rig and began to take core samples from the middle of the lake. Scott Anderson and his team from Northern Arizona University

Top: The soccer-ball-sized rocks around the Clay Mammoth were a real puzzle. *Bottom left:* Mastodon ribs were some of the most common fossils. *Bottom right:* Applying the first layer of plaster to the Clay Mammoth.

FIRST HUMANS, LAST MAMMOTH?

As little as 14,000 years ago, the American West was host to camels, tapirs, bison, horses, giant ground sloths, bear-sized beavers, caribou, short-faced bears, mastodons, mammoths, vultures, lions, saber-toothed cats, cheetahs, and dire wolves. Portions of North America looked like the Serengeti Plain in Africa. About 13,000 years ago, more than 30 species of large North American animals (also known as megafauna) went extinct in a very short time span. We are still trying to figure out what caused these extinctions. There are three main theories for the cause of the megafaunal extinctions: climatic change, human hunting, and disease .

Climate change undoubtedly played some role in causing the megafaunal extinction. With the end of the last glacial period between 21,000 and 11,500 years ago, climate and habitats radically changed. Winters were shortened, then lengthened, and then shortened again, with the opposite for summers. Rainfall patterns changed, causing food sources to be altered, which led to birthing cycles being disrupted. These changes almost certainly affected the range, size, and health of large animal populations.

The arrival of humans in North America may also have been central to the extinctions. The first humans in North America arrived on the continent before 13,800 years ago. They crossed the Bering Land Bridge during low sea level and hunted their way southward. As they moved, they encountered pristine prairies and woodlands teeming with game. They brought with them superb hunting technology consisting

of sophisticated dart-throwing tools called atlatls and razor-sharp fluted stone dart points. Many sites in the American West contain these tools along with the butchered remains of ice age animals. Overhunting of key species, probably mammoths and mastodons, may have caused a chain reaction leading to the collapse of ecosystems and the extinction of other animals.

Disease is a third plausible cause for megafaunal extinction, but it is a difficult hypothesis to test. Humans from the Asia had been living alongside animals for hundreds of thousands of years. Disease, passed back and forth between animals and humans, would have evolved, becoming more virulent and lethal at the same time the immune systems of humans and animals evolved to combat the diseases. When humans and animals migrated to North America, they may have brought with them diseases that simply overpowered the immune systems of the native megafauna, becoming a factor in their extinction.

All three theories likely explain part of the North American megafaunal extinction. Continued research on this extinction will help us understand what impact humans have on continent-scale ecosystems, how climate change and habitat loss can cause extinction, and what the future may hold for many large animals left on Earth.

Clovis points from the Dent mammoth kill site near Longmont, Colorado.

were taking very closely spaced samples for palynology so that they could reconstruct the vegetation of the lake as it filled in.

With that many scientists in camp, we were able to have interesting conversations about the future of our collective research on the site and who would do what. We were in amazing agreement for a bunch of scientists, and it was clear that the core team had done a really good job selecting a group who could work together.

On June 22 Doug Ziegler arrived on site for the first time. He came on the busiest day of the entire project, when we had more than 90 people working. Kit and Joe brought him down in the hole where more than 50 diggers were furiously eating through the remaining sediment. They set up a captain's chair so he could watch the massive dig. While he was there, we found the lower jaw of another baby mastodon.

We were also continuing work on the beach, measuring and sampling the logs. Ian bought a new chainsaw to slice up the 120,000-year-old logs. It seemed somehow disrespectful, but we didn't know what else to do. The week before, Steve Nash and Peter Brown, a tree-ring specialist, had sampled some logs with a chainsaw to see if they could reconstruct a dendrochronology (dating based on tree rings) for the lake. They were specialists, so it seemed like a reasonable approach. Besides, Ian really wanted to buy a new chainsaw. As we removed logs, we discovered that the bones we had seen protruding from under the logs were actually parts of a fairly complete mastodon skeleton. The bones weren't attached to each other, but they were close enough that we figured we were looking at a single animal. Here was a mastodon that had died and fallen apart on a beach. His bones hadn't slid into the lake. The find seemed to be another bit of evidence to support the shake-kill-pause-shake-bury hypothesis, except this animal had only made it to the shake-kill-pause phase.

On Friday night, June 24, we had an invigorating recap, and Richard Stucky brought a variety of small bones to dinner. He had a ziplock bag that contained an incredibly delicate bone about 2 inches long. Joe thought it was some sort of bird arm bone, but Dan had a different idea. He suggested that it was the finger bone of a bat. That was interest-

50 diggers and 27 scientists on site this week. We are learning lots fast. #iceagedig
22 June

Top: The USGS team cored the lake, storing the cylinders of sediment in plastic sleeves. *Middle:* Kirk shows Doug and Sharon Ziegler the lower jaw of a juvenile mastodon while Joe Enzer looks on. *Bottom:* Ian and Joe begin the bizarre process of sawing a 120,000-year-old log at the very bottom of the hole.

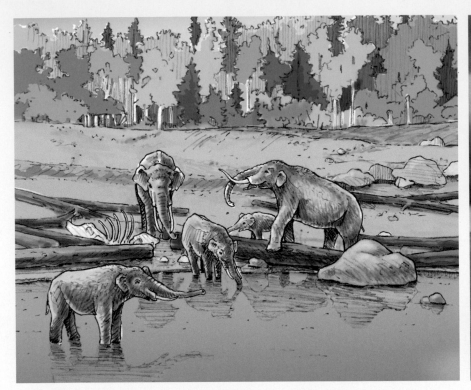

Left: A mastodon family mills about on the beach. One hypothesis is that they were killed when an earthquake turned the silt at their feet into quicksand. *Right:* The twice-found bat finger bone that turned out to be an arm bone of an ice age shore bird.

ing. After dinner, I put the bag in a little cardboard box with a few other bones and took it back to my condo.

Most of the crew went into Aspen that night to see Toots and the Maytals. I had seen that band nearly 30 years before, but I was now 30 years older and pretty bone tired after 42 days of digging, so I stayed at home and had a great night's sleep.

In the morning, I grabbed the cardboard box to take it to Carol's room to log its contents into the database. Carol's condo was the place where the daily load of bones was processed, and her dining room table was typically covered in mastodon bones. When I got there, I looked in the box and was surprised to see that the bag with the bat finger was missing. I retraced my steps back to my condo, but it was nowhere to be seen. I went back to the dining room to see if I had left it down there. Then I retraced my steps again. This time I emptied the garbage can, with no result. I was

getting desperate. Alice Steindler wandered in, and I enlisted her help. Soon, several other people were helping me look for the missing ziplock. I did not want to be the person who lost the only fossil bat from Snowmass.

After a full hour, I was beginning to think that I was that person. This was going to be pretty embarrassing. Then I heard distant shrieking. I ran outside and followed the sound to the bear-proof garbage locker. And there, in the Dumpster, was Alice holding the bat finger.

Alice had figured that someone cleaning the dining room had swept the bag with the bat finger into the trash and had taken the trash to the Dumpster. She had literally wallowed her way through every particle in the nearly full Dumpster and was just about to give up when the little bag emerged.

Alice smelled like Dumpster, but she and I were the happiest people in the Roaring Fork Valley at that moment. Later on it turned out that Joe was right and Dan was wrong—the bone did belong to a shorebird rather than a bat. I'm just glad we found it twice.

Week Seven: A Puddle or a Palace
SUNDAY, JUNE 26—SATURDAY, JULY 2, 2011

The final week of the dig moved rapidly toward the finish. We used two skid steers, the mini-excavator, and two track hoes to move dirt fast, pushing past the 6,000-yard mark. Bone production started to drop off simply because we were running out of fossil-rich sediment. We were back down to 100 bones a day, a sign that we were nearing the end.

Bryan and his crew struggled with the problem of the Clay Mammoth. Ian's dad, Jim, showed up and applied his contractor's brain to the problem. There was a lot of head-scratching and speculating, and everyone had an opinion on the best way to get a 5-ton block of clay from Snowmass to Denver. In the end, they trenched around the entire mammoth. Then Joe Sertich brought in a skid steer and ate away the outside of the trench so the mammoth now lay on top of a 4-foot-high pedestal of peat and clay. Bryan went to town and bought a bunch of big beams. Jim drove to Grand Junction three different times for various bolts and parts. Skinny interns #6 and #7 then dug beam-sized tunnels under the mammoth. Once eight tunnels were dug, they pushed the beams through and, with a bottle jack on either end of each beam, jacked them up to equal levels. With the beams now bearing weight, they dug out the space between each beam and slid in a section of plywood level with the beams and nail-gunned them in place. Then they bolted a composite beam made of vertical planks to each side of the block, connecting all the cross beams. Finally, they covered the entire block with plaster and burlap. This job took the better part of a week, and now they needed to figure out how to lift this massive block. Joe Enzer started calling crane companies.

Charles Nelson excavates a bison jawbone.

More plaster goes onto the Clay Mammoth.

Digging the trench around the Clay Mammoth.

Clearing space around the Clay Mammoth.

Intern Hannah O'Neill tunnels between the beams.

All eight beams are in place and up on bottle jacks.

The beams are connected, and the Clay Mammoth is ready to be lifted with a crane.

Carlos helped us dig our way up the slope toward the pair of porta-potties on the road. This was some of the last remaining undug dirt. There were fewer fossils than we expected in these layers, so we were able to use heavy equipment. But more logs appeared as we pursued the ancient beach into the hillside. On June 27 Carlos's bucket dragged across the top of a huge mastodon skull. It was in the uppermost debris flow, above the Beach Mastodon and just below the porta-potties. As we dug, the skull bones began to appear, really big bones, and lots of them. With only a few days to go, we had found the largest mastodon of the entire dig. Like the Beach Mastodon, this one was a fairly complete skeleton, with its bones scattered over a fairly small area. Another animal stuck at shake-kill-pause. Because of his location, we named him Portaleu (with a French pronunciation).

With only four days to go to the official deadline, the discovery of a massive mastodon skeleton should have shaken us, but we were so used to pulling bones out of the ground that it didn't even faze us. Team P jacketed his massive skull and his 6-foot-wide pelvis. We bagged ribs, limb bones, and vertebrae. I found his intact jawbone. And all of this occurred within 20 feet of our paired porta-potties.

By June 29 Jim and Bryan had fully rigged the Clay Mammoth. We all took bets on how much the massive pile of wood, plaster burlap, clay, peat, and mammoth weighted. I guessed 10,000 pounds since it was such a nice round number.

After lunch, a couple of SUVs emerged out of the woods from the direction of the Zieglers' house. I had heard that the Zieglers' next-door neighbor was Michael Eisner, the former CEO of Paramount and the Walt Disney Company, and I wondered if he might show up on site at some point. As a paleontologist (who is often confused for an archaeologist), I have to give credit to the Indiana Jones movies. More so than *Jurassic Park, Raiders of the Lost Ark* revived the icon of the adventurous scientist. People will often introduce me as the Indiana Jones of Denver. I don't carry a whip or a handgun, and I am embarrassed by the reference, but I love the fact that this movie made people think about the prehistoric mysteries of the world around them. Eisner ran Paramount when this series came out in 1981, and here he was on the site. Wandering around with him and his family and friends, it was cool to watch him be amazed by a major discovery in his backyard.

Top: Trying to visualize how much dirt we actually moved by hand is really difficult. Professional excavators measure the volume of material they move in cubic yards. One cubic yard of silt weighs 1.1 tons. We moved 7,000 yards, or 8,000 tons, or more than 800 dump truck loads of dirt. This volume of dirt is equivalent to the illustrated cube of dirt 60 feet on a side. *Lower left:* Intense thunderstorms caused the entire crew to squeeze into our small job trailer. *Lower right:* Krista Williams and Carol Lucking sorting supplies in front of the tool container.

ICE AGE CLIMATE CYCLES

The only constant about climate on Earth is that it is always changing. Many factors drive climate change, but a central agent throughout earth's history is carbon: the more atmospheric carbon, the warmer the planet; the less atmospheric carbon, the cooler the planet. Carbon is special because not only does it form a greenhouse gas (carbon dioxide) in the atmosphere, but it is also incorporated into all life on earth, is dissolved in the oceans, and mixes with rain and snow to form a weak acid that is a very important agent of erosion. In fact, the cycle of carbon through life, air, water, and rock dictates the major, long-term trends in global warming and cooling.

Even though it might not feel like it on a hot summer day, we live in an ice age that began 2.6 million years ago. This ice age has had cold glacial periods and warmer interglacial periods like the one we are in today. Before the present ice age, the last time that the planet had as much ice as it does today was about 300 million years ago. The periods between ice ages are commonly called greenhouse periods and during these times there is little or no ice anywhere on earth. Carbon is responsible for the major change between the greenhouse and the icehouse world. Overprinted onto these two climate states are shorter, climate cycles driven by celestial mechanics.

During the First World War, geophysicist Milutin Milankovitch, while in an Austrian jail, developed a theory that described the collective effects of changes in Earth's movements upon its climate. In particular, Milankovitch argued that variations in eccentricity, axial tilt, and precession of Earth's orbit determined climatic patterns on Earth by changing the amount of sunlight that hits the Northern Hemisphere. Milankovitch Cycles were difficult to prove until the international deep-sea coring project was undertaken. In 1976, a paper on deep-sea cores entitled "Variations in the Earth's Orbit: Pacemaker of the Ice Ages" sealed the argument that celestial mechanics play a major role in short-term climate change. These short-term changes are felt most acutely when Earth is an icehouse.

About 2.6 million years ago, Earth entered a full icehouse climate state, or ice age, driven by the reduction of carbon in the atmosphere. Within this ice age, the climate has changed from glacial states with lots of ice to interglacial states with less ice. Today we live in an interglacial period called the Holocene. This pattern of lots of ice and less ice is driven by the Milankovitch Cycles.

The change between glacials and interglacials is dramatic. Over the last 2.6 million years there have been more than 20 shifts between these climate states. During our last glacial period, which reached its maximum about 21,000 years ago, as much as 2.5 miles of ice was sitting on Canada. This ice sheet spread down into the United States and carved out Puget Sound and the Great Lakes, and pushed a pile of rock to form Long Island. If you stood in southern Illinois and looked north, you would have seen a mountain of ice sloping away from you and eventually rising more than 10,000 feet into the sky. By 11,000 years ago, most of this ice had melted away, exposing the Great Plains of central North America.

The Snowmass site allows us to look at the Illinoian glaciation, the Sangamon interglacial, and the Wisconsin glaciation. It sets the stage for our own interglacial period, the Holocene, which began about 11,500 years. By preserving parts of two glacials and an interglacial at high elevation, this site has tremendous potential to help scientists understand the impacts of climate change in the Colorado Rockies.

An elderly gentleman with Eisner was having a hard time moving around, so we didn't walk down into the pit where most of the digging was going on. Instead, we stood at the top of the rim and looked down on the teams of happy diggers. I took the moment to meet the people in Eisner's group and learned that this guy was Frank Gehry, the renowned architect. The site was getting more interesting by the day.

A thunderstorm roared over the lip of the moraine, and it started to pour rain. The Eisner party ran for their cars and drove off. Lightning bolts started to strike nearby, and Ian yelled for everyone to run for the shelter of the trailer. We packed 45 people into the small trailer and waited out the storm.

A longtime colleague of mine named Bob Raynolds had come up from Denver to see the site and spent a day with us. Bob is a perplexing character with a big altruistic brain and some unusual superhuman skills. For example, he can put a Styrofoam cup of coffee on his dashboard and drive down a rough and rocky road without spilling a drop. He can go for days without food or water. But mainly, he is a real big-picture guy, and I shudder when he is around because I know he will see things, big things, that I have missed. After 47 days, I thought we had pretty much sorted this site out. We had dug our dirt and saved all of the fossils. There was no fossil left behind. We had done right by this amazing world-class site and were going to finish on time so that the Snowmass Water and Sanitation District could fulfill their commitment to their customers, taxpayers, and the Zieglers. We had saved the fossils, Kit Hamby would have his water, and Doug Ziegler would have his lake. We were going to deliver a win-win-win situation. I was feeling good.

The happy team hoists a log from the beach.

Top left: Interns Hannah O'Neill and Kaitlin Stanley hang around the trailer after plastering Portaleu's pelvis. *Bottom left:* Tim Seeber and Malcolm Bedell with Portaleu's femur. *Above:* Joe Burr, son of Hudick foreman Kevin Burr, holding the fossil femur of a bullfrog that he found while sitting on a pile of dirt and watching his dad work. *Opposite:* Paul Vallejos with Portaleu's tibia.

Bob spent the day wandering around the site, drawing little pictures in his notebook and chatting with the diggers. He is more of a thinker than a digger, and I could see his mind working. That night, like every night, we had our daily recap. The captains told of their accomplishments and praised their teams. I dissed the captains and praised the diggers. Everyone was feeling good.

Bob pulled me aside and asked me, "Why are you letting this world-class site get flooded beneath a reservoir? You know that this place is really sig-

nificant. You know that it has the potential to be a national monument or a World Heritage site. Why are you letting it drown on your watch?" He had a point, and it knocked the shine off my penny. Other people had asked the same question over the past seven weeks, but I had been so focused on my triple win that I hadn't confronted the issue head on.

I decided to bring the matter to a group discussion. We had 57 people at dinner that night, so we certainly had a quorum. Prompted by Bob's challenge, I asked the group, "Are we doing the right thing? It has always felt like the right thing to me, but are we missing the bigger picture? Is this site larger than all of us? Should we, in the 11th hour, change our tactics and fight the completion of the reservoir and lobby for the creation of a national monument?"

That started a conversation all right. For the next two hours we had one of the most interesting and inspiring conversations I can ever remember. Everyone participated, and it was clear that this issue had been lying just below the surface for many. At one point Bob asked the group, "There are other places to store water—do you want a puddle or a palace?"

As the conversation went on, I was beginning to feel sick. I couldn't imagine reversing directions and betraying all of the solid relationships that I had worked so hard to forge. I talked less and listened more, and I watched the argument take a fascinating turn. Jeff Pigati, the USGS scientist who had become the central geologist of the project, pointed out that the amazing preservation of the fossils was a function of their lack of exposure to oxygen. Leaving the site open would guarantee its eventual destruction. This site was not like Porky Hansen's discovery in Hot Springs, South Dakota—it could not take long-term exposure to the air. The best way to preserve the site was to cap it with clay and cover it with water. The triple win had won the night and the air was cleared for us to finish the dig.

We spent the next two days digging the last of the silt out of the bottom of the pit. By July 1, the deadline, we had cleared the silt all the way down to the top of the moraine and we were in clean-up mode. One of the last fossils to be found was the partial skull and perfect tusk of a little baby mastodon. Down to the bitter end, the site was taunting us with its peculiar past.

The pelvis of Portaleu and the massive Clay Mammoth block were the only fossils left on the site. We had moved 7,000 yards of dirt—mostly by hand—in only seven weeks. The deadline had come and we were done. We left the site at 6 p.m. and headed back to the condos for the last supper. Intern #2 made a chocolate pudding with the precise stratigraphy of the reservoir. Emotional speeches were made. Later that night, we had a big party on the site and built a bonfire of wooden pallets. The best dig ever was over.

Below left: Carol Lucking appreciates Lesley Petrie's stratigraphically accurate Ziegler Reservoir pudding. *Top right:* A celebratory intern pyramid. *Below right:* A bonfire to celebrate a dig well dug. *Opposite:* The Zulu shovel army. Our exhilaration always exceeded our exhaustion.

CODA

Of course, it wasn't really over. The science was just beginning. Most of the crew departed on July 2, but 14 of us stayed on to deal with the million little details that had to be nailed down before we headed home ourselves. And of course we realized that even though July 1 was the deadline, the construction crews wouldn't start working until after the Fourth of July weekend, so we had a couple more days to poke around the site and make sure we were really done.

On the morning of July 4, and on the spur of the moment, we decided that we needed to be part of Aspen's traditional Fourth of July parade. We checked their website and discovered that we'd needed to apply for a permit a week in advance, but we figured that we could show up with some bones and talk our way into the lineup. Joe and I drove Big Blue into town where the parade was being assembled. Sure enough, a wink from

Joe and a chance to touch a real mastodon bone convinced the parade organizer to ignore our lack of permit. We were in thick traffic about 100 yards behind the giant bicycle mammoth that the late inventor Nick DeWolf had built for the 2002 Burning Man event. A bunch of his friends were planning to pedal it in the parade. We figured that we had to do this parade together. After all, when was the last time that mammoths and mastodons were legitimate participants in an Aspen parade? Ignoring the officials who tried to keep us in line, we crept slowly ahead, jumping our way forward until we were able to pull in right behind the big beast. One by one, our crew members emerged out of the crowd and climbed onto the truck. We shared hard hats and museum vests with the mammoth bike crew. We hoisted our giant bones as the parade started. It was amazing to watch people watch us. Everybody had heard about the dig.

Opposite left: Joe Sertich shares a real mastodon femur with a real horseman. *Opposite right:* Big Blue and a load of very happy diggers and their bones. *Left:* Alice Steindler and Jim Miller were yelling and screaming throughout the entire parade. *Right:* Museum president George Sparks supported his team by walking the entire parade route. *Below:* The Mammoth Quadrocycle takes a corner in downtown Aspen.

Nobody could believe that we had brought the real bones. Again and again, people yelled from the crowd, "Are they real?" We yelled back, "They are real! Yes, they are real!"

The next week, I flew back to Aspen from Denver to watch the hoisting of the clay mammoth block with Governor Hickenlooper and his 9-year old son, Teddy. The 50-ton crane lifted the 5-ton block onto a trailer, which then headed to Denver. Two flatbeds full of 75 plaster jackets had already arrived. The museum swung into action, drying and preserving the bones. We left Cody Newton, a lone archaeologist, on site for the next two months to watch the project and keep an eye out for stray bones as Kit and Joe Enzer and the Hudick guys built their dam. The dam was completed on October 19, and water started flowing into it the next day. As a final gesture, Kit had built a gravel road down to the floor of the lake on the off chance that we would come back for another round of bone digging.

As I sit here, writing this last page on November 29, 2011, it's hard to believe that only 13½ months have elapsed since Jesse's dozer tumbled those ribs. In that time, we ran 69 days of full-scale excavation that involved more than 380 diggers who delivered more than 3,245 person-days of effort. Those 7,000 yards of dirt worked out to more than 20,000,000 pounds, and the final bone count of fall plus spring ended up at over 5,426. This was one of the largest and fastest digs in North American history.

Water is flowing out of East Snowmass Creek, and Ziegler Reservoir will be full by next spring. The town of Snowmass Village is pondering its luck and wondering how mastodons and mammoths will change its future. Back at the Denver Museum of Nature & Science, our crew is working like beavers: cleaning, drying, cataloging, studying, and beginning to display this phenomenal trove of ice age information. The team of scientists has now grown to more than 45. They are all busily doing their parts to make sense of this find and working to document their discoveries in scientific publications. National Geographic has completed its documentary, which addresses the still unanswered questions about mastodon mass death and the true story of the Clay Mammoth. With an election year looming, climate change has all but completely disappeared from public conversation, yet carbon dioxide in the atmosphere continues to climb. Colorado now has a world-class high-elevation fossil site that will be part of its history forever. The record of its ancient climate is locked in the mud of Ziegler Reservoir, but now that mud is in the laboratories of a dozen universities and its secrets are starting to be revealed.

I wonder what Jesse Steele is digging today.

Left: Governor John Hickenlooper and Carlos Mendoza discuss the finer points of mammoth hoisting. *Right:* Governor Hickenlooper and Ian Miller watch the successful lifting of the 10,000-pound Clay Mammoth block.

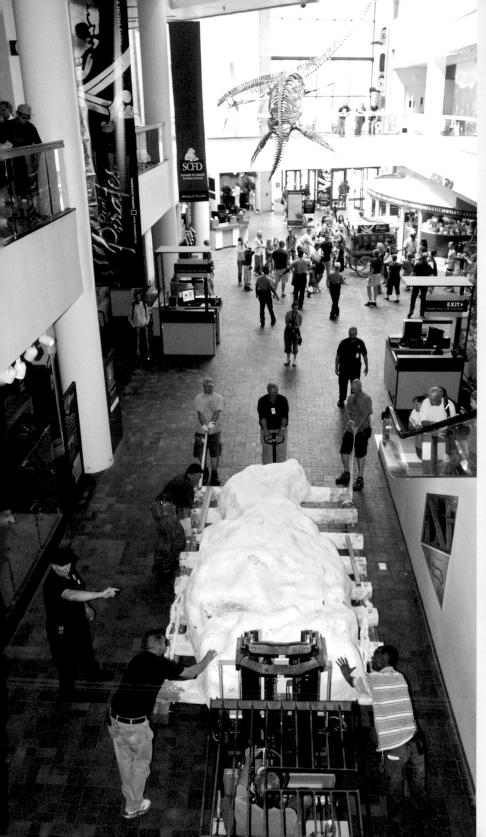

Left: The Clay Mammoth being wheeled into place at the Denver Museum of Nature & Science. *Top:* Back in the conservation laboratory, each specimen received its own plastic bag and the drying began. *Bottom:* We were surprised and delighted to learn that Kit Hamby had built a gravel road into the bottom of the completed reservoir, keeping open the possibility of future fossil excavations.

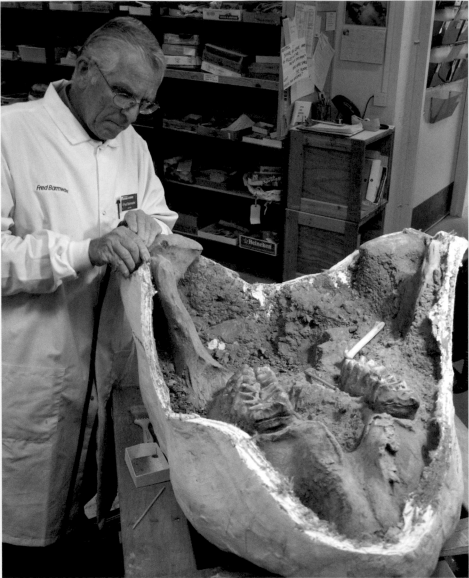

Top left: Heather Finlayson and Sharon Von Broembsen apply tape to keep glue joints in place while they set. *Bottom left:* Fritz Koether exposes a mastodon tusk. *Above:* Fred Barmwater removes matrix from the massive lower jaw of Portaleu, the last mastodon of the dig. *Opposite:* Billy Kinneer exposes bone with a paint brush.

Three claws from Jefferson's ground sloths.

An essentially perfect lower jaw from a mastodon.
Note the pair of mandibular (chin) tusks.

A massive mammoth tooth.

A portion of a bison jaw.

Two views of a mastodon thoracic vertebra.

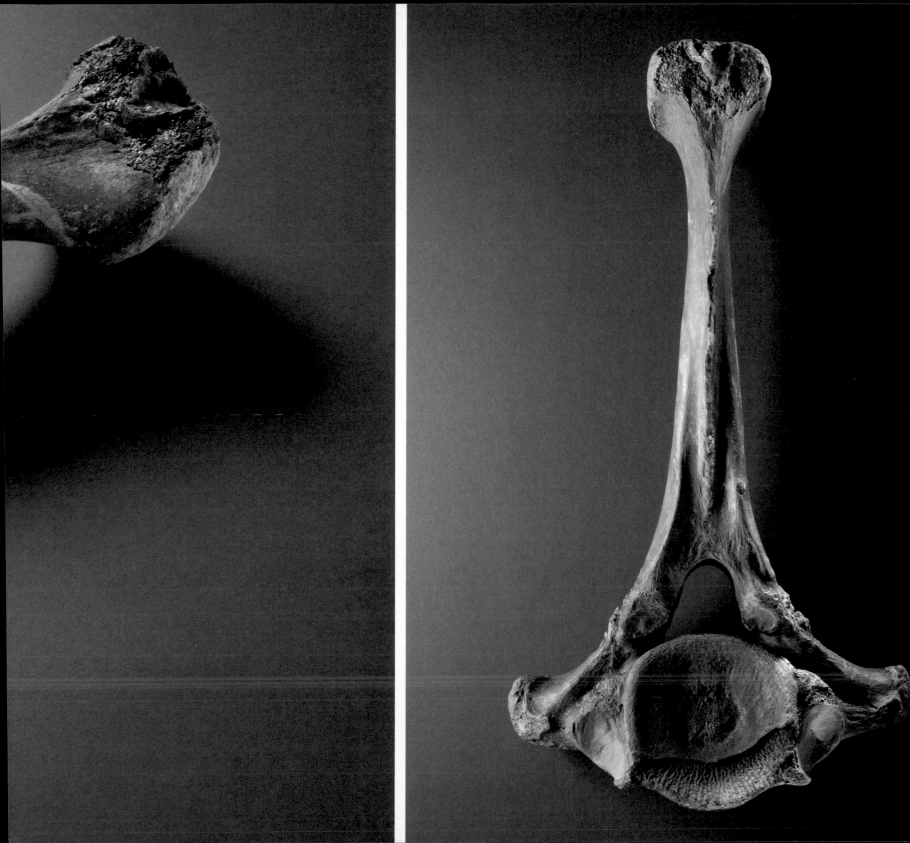

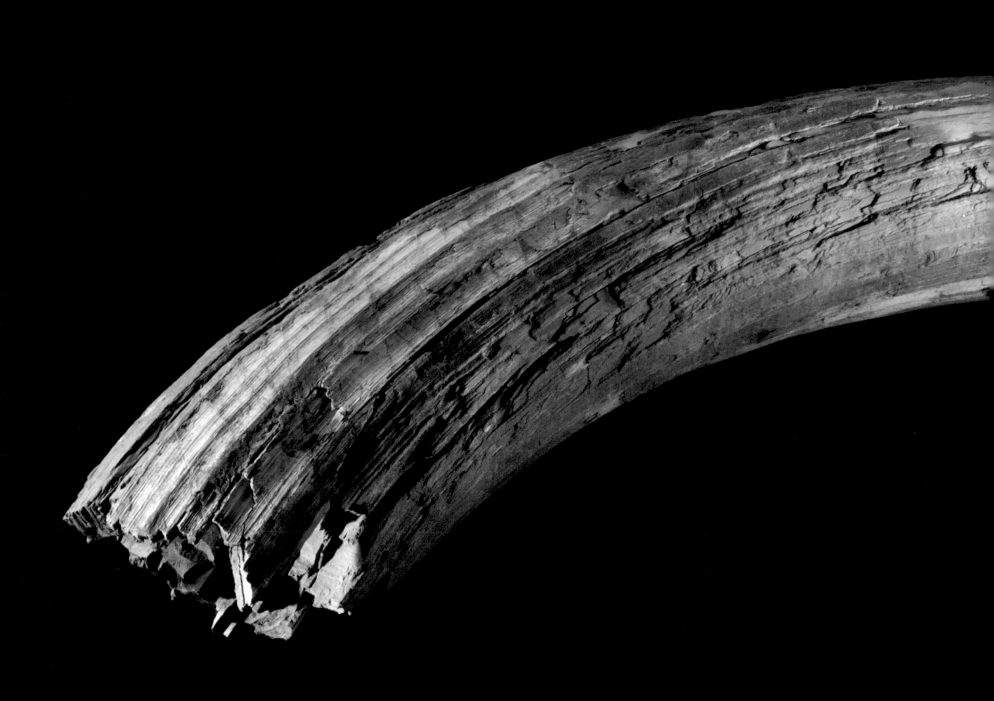

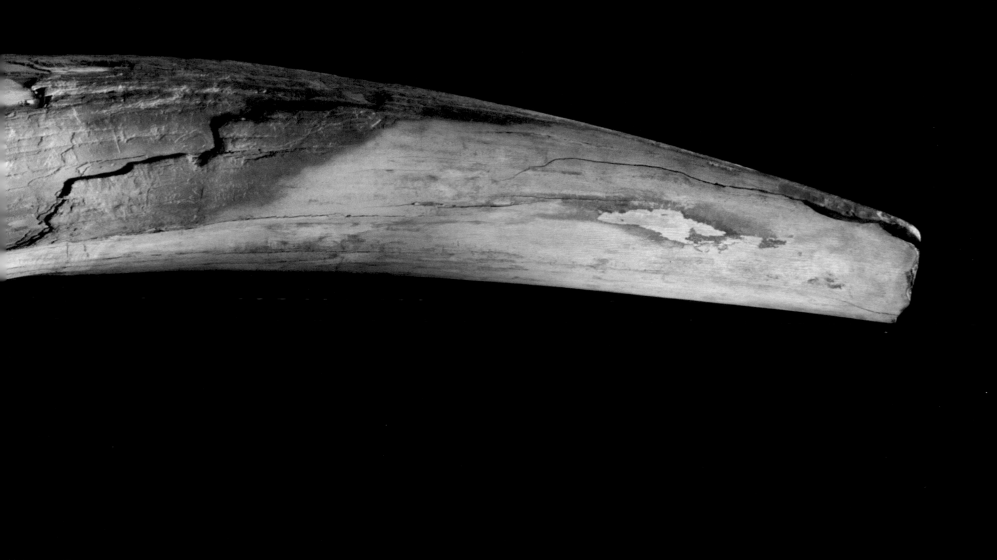

This gorgeous mastodon tusk was one of the
three discovered on October 28, 2010.

ACKNOWLEDGMENTS

The Snowmastodon Project was a success due to the cooperative and enthusiastic efforts of more than 1,000 people. As they say, it takes a village; in this case, it was Snowmass Village. We are deeply grateful to everyone who was involved in this once-in-a-lifetime experience. We have tried to list everyone who played a role, and we apologize to those we may have missed. It was incredibly fun getting to know so many people in such a short, sweet time.

Snowmass Water and Sanitation District: Jane Campbell Baker, Rhonda Bazil, Gretchen Stock Bell, John Bell, Dave Dawson, Christy Duckett, Brad Elrod, Joe Enzer, Jeremy Everding, Joe Farrell III, Sam Flores, Ashley Hamby, Debbie Hamby, Jenny Hamby, Kit Hamby, Mark Hamilton, Jim Lottig, Carlos Mendoza, Jose Munoz, Dennis Palardy, Ruben Salas, Debbie Shore, Michael P. Shore, Doug Throm, Randy Urban.

Gould Construction Inc.: Ricardo Abad, Dean Bradley, Mark Duerr, Wayne Eichler, David Gyolai, Brett Gould, Evan Gould, Mark Gould, Mark Gould Jr., Nick Hermosillo, Eric Hodera, Donald Hubbard, James Hylton, Paul Jacobson, Jon Jeffryes, Kyle Johnson, Jerry Kivett, Jeramy Mann, Charles McClees, James Meraz, Tony Miller, Josh Moylan, Alan Noland, Kent & Wendi Olson, Brenda Ruppert, Jose Santillan, Jesse Steele, Richard Weinheimer, Denver Wilkin-Mondiekis.

The Ziegler Family: Cherrie & Tom Catlin, Josie Norris, Cindy Ziegler-Fritz & Tom Fritz, Debbie Ziegler & Jim Gluek, Doug & Sharon Ziegler, Faith Ziegler & Tim Sullivan, Heidi Ziegler & David Vollmar, Missy Ziegler, Peter & Joan Ziegler, R. Scott & Yvonne Ziegler.

Town of Snowmass Village: Bill Boineau, Lesley Compagnone, Russell Forrest, TOSV Town Council.

State of Colorado: Kevin Black, Rep. Laura Bradford, Gov. John Hickenlooper, Teddy Hickenlooper, Garrett Jackson, Ed Nichols, Kirk Russell, Sen. Gail Schwartz, Richard Wilshusen.

Hudick Excavating Inc.: Kevin & Joe Burr, Zane Hudick, Jim Prudhomme, James Simon, Rob Warne.

URS Corporation: Dale Baures, Craig Helm, Dave Lady, Bob Mutaw, John Nicholl, Lea Anne Russell, John Sikora.

W. W. Wheeler Engineering Inc.: Steve Jamieson, Don Lopez, Steve Maly.

SurvCo Inc.: Samuel Phelps.

R + R Engineers-Surveyors Inc.: Bob Rickard, David MacDonald.

Aspen Skiing Company: Matt Hamilton, Mike Kaplan, John Rigney, Rachel Schaefer, Auden Schendler.

Snowmass Tourism: Beth Albert, Susan Hamley, Emily Johnson, Patsy Popejoy, Sue Whittingham.

Top of the Village Condominiums: Marie Kastener, Dave Spence, TOV team.

Aspen Historical Society: Nina Gabianelli, Lisa Hancock, Georgia Hanson.

The Aspen Institute: Cristal Logan, Amy Margerum.

Aspen Center for Environmental Studies: Ellen Burns, Tom Cardamone, Nick Carter, Jamie Cundiff, Jim Kravitz, Adam McCurdy, Sarah Schmidt, Anda Rojs Smalls, Rebecca Weiss.

Ice Age Discovery Committee (Tusk Force): Chuck Barth, Rhonda Bazil, Valerie Borthwick, Lesley Compagnone, Colleen Doyle, Russell Forrest, Susan Hamley, Lisa Hancock, Georgia Hanson, Sandy Jackson, Stan Kornasiewicz, John Rigney, Sarah Schmidt, Gail Schwartz, Anda Rojs Smalls, Julie Ann Woods.

Ice Age Discovery Center Volunteers: Cassia Boyd, Jacki Boyer, Ron Carsten, Tom Clapper, Diana Conrad, Reine Fedor, Arlene Ginn, Barbara Goldstein, Kim Hartman, Beth Hayden, Marcee Hobbs, Ali Jackson, Walt Krom, Carolyn Purvis, Jack Rafferty, Julie Riggins, Jean Ringwalt, Joann Rodden, Christopher Ryerson, Georgeann Waggaman, Gayle Weiss, Marla Welch, Lisa Wilkinson.

The Roaring Fork Teacher-Diggers: Trent Bakich, Andrea Brogan, Diana Buirgy, James Campbell, Ron Carsten, Chris Faison, Sandy Jackson, Lisa Lawrence, Charlie Leech, Georgina Levey, Kristin Lidman, Sarah Schmidt, Greg Shaffran, Alice Steindler, Patrick Uphus, Andre Wille.

Colorado Mountain College Students: James Callahan, Alex Curtiss, Ronald Hendricks, Wade Hutt, Bryan Schrimmer.

Snowmastodon Team Captains: Lisa Delonay & Krista Williams (fall and spring admin captains), Heather Finlayson (Team Tiger Salamander captain), Laura Holtman & Heather Hope (fall and spring media captains), Carol Lucking (data captain), Meghan McFarlane & Jude Southward (bone-washing captains), Paula Meadows (HR captain), Liz Miller (breakfast captain), Dane Miller (Team Trench captain), Samantha Richards (outreach captain), Jodi Schoemer (Snowmastodon project manager & Ice Age Discovery Center captain), Joe Sertich (Team Sloth captain), Bryan Small (Team Mammoth captain), Josh Smith (Team P captain), George Sparks (captain of captains), Richard Stucky & Dena Meade-Hunter (screen wash captains), Shelley Thompson (fund-raising captain), Rick Wicker (camera captain), Jim Cornette, Steve Wagner, Fritz Koether (volunteer captains).

Interns 1–9: Corinna Troll (1), Lesley Petrie (2), Kaitlin Stanley (3), Tyler Kerr (4), Brittany Grimm (5), Adam Freierman (6), Hannah O'Neill (7), Nathaniel Fox (8), Gussie Maccracken (9).

DMNS Staff Who Worked on the Snowmastodon Project in Denver and Snowmass (if not mentioned above): Julie Abbott, Polly Andrews, Amanda Avram, Beth Bavolek, Dave Baysinger, Amanda Bennett, Dave Blumenstock, Mitchell Blystone, Mary Jane Bradbury, Carla Bradmon, Garrett Briggs, Matt Brownell, Dean Buffo, Rich Busch, Mary Bushbaum, James Calder, Julia Calle, Colleen Carter, Christie Cass, Jacqueline Close, Connor Coleman, Presley Conkle, Liz Cook, Bridget Coughlin, Dave Cuomo, Liz Davis, Nicole Dondelinger, Beth Ellis, Kim Evans, Sonny Evans, Jessica Fletcher, Jess Fox, Sandi Garcia, Matt Gargan, Nicole Garneau, Tracy Glass-McKenna, Eddie Goldstein, Kelly Goulette, Kathie Gully, Mary Hacking, Kris Haglund, Whitey Hagadorn, Veronika Hall, Maria Hannon, Elaine Harkins, Karen Hays, Steve Holen, Ian Holtum,

Above: A bucket of grade-A interns. *Below:* The team captains worked the entire 51 days and led the project to success: (left to right) Joe Sertich, Meghan McFarlane, Dane Miller, Josh Smith, Bryan Small, Kirk Johnson, Ian Miller, Heather Finlayson, Carol Lucking.

Michon Scott, Raymond Scott, Eytan Sharton-Bierig, John Shinton, Becky Shorey, Leslie Simpson, Mary Stewart, Misty Swan, Susan Tablack, Janice Tang, Lou Taylor, Thomas Toft, William Vigor, Sharon Von Broembsen, David & Shirley Warren, Linda Weiss, Karen Whiteley, Jean Widman, Jeanne Wilson, Sharon Wolfe, Robert Zogg.

DMNS Curation Volunteers: Moriah Fremd, Ginny Hoyle, Mark & Dena Hunter, Jill Malley, Giovanna Mendoza, Christine & Clayton Powers, Cynthia Russell, Eliza Stein, James Sundine, Olivia Verma, Kate Zubin-Stathopoulus.

DMNS Program Volunteers: Ashley Affleck-Johnson, Connie Bender, Katie Blaser, Tom Brightwell Jackie Brinkham, Gerry Bunce, Diana Busik, Becky Cottrell, Frances Davison, Marilyn Ellis, Gretchen Frank, Lauren Frye, Karen Hall, Theresa Halsey, Kathryn Harhai, Bonnie Hegge, Gloria Hershberger, Madeleine James, Dillon McGreevy, Cindy & Bill Kaelber, Vicky Mateev, Cathy McAllister, Jean Millar, Tobie Miller, Lael Moe, Barb Morrison, Julie & Murph Murphy, Peg O'Connor, Marcia Ornstein, Toni Prante, Cathie Quering-Barnes, Ellen Roth, Priscilla & Tammie Sawicki, Riley Scadden, Don Schuderer, Lisa Seiler, Pat Taylor, Liz Tokheim, Arlene Solof, Mary Venner, Bill Vigor, Ralph Wagner, Waldo Wedel, Barry Weiss, Penny Wisdom, Adrienne Young.

Snowmastodon Science Team: The science team has grown to 41 members and now includes: Tom Ager, Scott Anderson, Richard Baker, Jordan Bright, Peter Brown, Bruce Bryant, Paul Carrara, Michael Cherney, Les Cwynar, John Demboski, Scott Elias, Dan Fisher, Russ Graham, Elizabeth Hadley, Kirk Hansen, Steve Holen, Jeff Honke, Steve Jackson, Gonzalo Jimenez-Moreno, Kirk Johnson, Nat Lifton, Shannon Mahan, Greg McDonald, Dane Miller, Ian Miller, Dan Muhs, Steve Nash, Cody Newton, Jim Paces, Jeff Pigati, Hendrik Poinar, Dave Porinchu, Adam Rountrey, Joe Sertich, Beth Shapiro, Saxon Sharpe, Sarah Spaulding, Mathias Stiller, Joseph Street, Laura Strickland,

Richard Stucky. We would like to especially thank the U.S. Geological Survey, which not only provided key personnel to the project but also covered costs of their analyses and staff.

Additional Participating Scientists: Stephen Char, Monika Dzieciatkowska, Harrison Gray, Peter & Cath Griffiths, Ryan Hill, Cristina M. Lugo-Centeno, Eugene S. Schweig, Cory Stephens.

People's Press: Holly Bornemeier, Catherine Lutz, Mirte Mallory, Jen Moss, Erin Rigney, Mark Stevens, George Stranahan, Craig Wheeless.

Readers: Betsy Armstrong, Chase DeForest, Kit Hamby, Heather Hope, Carol Lucking, Steve Nash, Jeff Pigati, George Sparks, Richard Stucky.

National Geographic: Cindy Aitken, John Bredar, Maryanne G. Culpepper, Laura Fravel, Eleanor Grant, Andrew Grimes, Bradley Hague, Danya Hakeem, Becky Hale, David Linstrom, Malvina Martin, Barbara Moffet, Kevin Padden, Howard Shack, Jamie Shreve, Clif Weins, Susan Welchman, Pam Wells, Rachel Whisenant.

NOVA: Paula Apsell, Evan Hadingham.

Financial Support: Funding for the Snowmastodon Project was provided by 591 organizations and individuals. Fund-raising parties were thrown for the Snowmastodon Project by Donna Dilanni & Pete Rispoli, Buz & Sherri Koelbel, Rob & Elaine LeBuhn, Susan & Lee McIntire, Karen & Donald (& Eric) Ringsby, and Jack & Viki Thompson. The staff and board of the Aspen Community Foundation managed the Snowmastodon Fund.

Contributions at the $25,000 and Higher Level: Anonymous, William & Elisabeth Armstrong, Aspen Skiing Company Family Fund, Montgomery Cleworth, Lester Crown, the Crown Family, Peter & Cathy Dea, Grogan Family Fund, Harvey Family Foundation, Leslie Liedtke, National Geographic Society, Quinette Family Fund, Ed & Jackie Warner, the Ziegler Family.

Contributions at the $10,000–24,999 Level: Butler Family Fund, Charles & Luanne Hazelrigg, Kenneth King Foundation, National Science Foundation (EAR-1125579, Program officers: Lisa Park Boush & Rich Lane), Slater Foundation, Michael & Iris Smith, A. R. Wilfley & Sons, Eleanore Wilfley.

Contributions at the $1,000–9,999 Level: Anonymous, Beth Archibald, Thomas & Cherrie Catlin, Isa Catto & Daniel Shaw, Tom & Noel Congdon, John Donnell, Charles Farver, Alan Fox, Lynn & Foster Friess Family Endowment Stewardship, Trish Green, Oliver & Lindsay Hickel, Michael Jefferson, Perry Peine, James Peterson, G. Roush, Rudge Foundation, Spidell Foundation, John Stockwell, Curt & Fleur Strand, Jack Wold, John Woodward, Peter & Joan Ziegler.

Contributions below $1,000: Thank you to the 548 generous donors at this level.

Finally: Special thanks to Harvie Branscomb, curator of the Nick DeWolf 2002 Burning Man mammoth quadrocycle; Jim Calaway; John & Carrie Morgridge; Doug Price; Michael Rosenfeld; Vaughn & Lori Shafer; Susan Tedeschi & Derek Trucks and the Tedeschi Trucks Band; and Kirk and Ian's very fabulous wives, Chase DeForest and Robyn Rissman.

GLOSSARY

Blade runners: staff and volunteers who worked with the bulldozer operators by following the blade at the front of the machine and watching for bones.

Bull Lake glaciation: the penultimate glaciation in the Rocky Mountains, between about 200,000 and 130,000 years ago; correlates to the Illinoian Stage in North America.

Cosmogenic dating: a suite of methods used to date how long a rock has been at the surface by quantifying the accumulation of isotopes produced by cosmic rays.

Debris flow: a very fast and dangerous land slide event that involves the movement of rock, soil, and water downhill.

Dendrochronology: the method of dating trees by counting their annual rings.

Ecosystem: the organization of interactions between plants, animals, and their environment in a region.

Fauna: the group of animals that live in a particular area.

Geochronology: the branch of geology focused on dating events in Earth's history.

Glacial period: the portion of an ice age between interglacial periods in which continents are covered by ice.

Ice age: Cold periods in Earth's history in which ice covers much of the land surface at high latitudes. Ice ages have cold glacial periods and warm interglacial periods.

Interglacial period: the portion of an ice age between glacial periods with warmer climate and less ice.

La Brea tar seeps: a series of tar deposits that trapped thousands of ice age animals in what would become downtown Los Angeles.

Mandible: the bone of the lower jaw.

Megafauna: the large-bodied animals of a fauna.

Microfauna: the little creatures in a fauna.

Moraine: a ridge of poorly sorted rock, sand, and clay pushed into a pile by a glacier.

Mountain Dragon: a restaurant and bar on the mall in Snowmass Village, Colorado.

Optically stimulated luminescence: a method used to date sediments by quantifying the time since that sediment was last exposed to sunlight.

Palynology: the study of live and fossil spores and pollen grains.

Pinedale glaciation: the most recent glaciation in the Rocky Mountains, between about 75,000 and 11,500 years ago; correlates to the Wisconsin Stage in North America.

Pleistocene epoch: the time beginning approximately 2.6 million years ago and ending 11,500 years ago, characterized by widespread glacial ice and the advent of modern humans.

Proboscidean: the order of animals with a flexible trunk, large tusks, a massive body, and columnar legs; includes the elephant and the now-extinct mammoth and mastodon.

Radiocarbon dating: a method used to date the age of organic materials by measuring the remaining amount of radioactive carbon in that material.

Sangamon interglacial: the warm period that lasted from 130,000 to 75,000 years ago and occurred between the Wisconsin and Illinioan glacial periods.

SELECTED READINGS

Bardoe, Cheryl. *Mammoths and Mastodons: Titans of the Ice Age.* New York: Abrams, 2010. 43 p.
> A kids' book with great science and pictures.

Bryant, Bruce. Geologic Map of the Highland Peak Quadrangle, Pitkin County, Colorado. U.S. Geological Survey map GQ-932. 1972.
> This is the geologic map that first mapped Ziegler Reservoir as an ice age lake.

Bryant, Bruce, and Peter L. Martin. "The Geologic Story of the Aspen Region: Mines, Glaciers, and Rocks." *U.S. Geological Survey Bulletin* #1603. 1988. 53 p.
> A good overview of the geology of Snowmass Village and environs.

Flannery, Tim F. *The Eternal Frontier: An Ecological History of North America and Its Peoples.* New York: Grove Press, 2002. 432 p.
> A great book about how North America got and lost its big mammals.

Guthrie, R. Dale. *Frozen Fauna of the Mammoth Steppe: The Story of Blue Babe.* Chicago: University of Chicago Press, 1990. 323 p.
> Guthrie describes the challenges of understanding ice age mammals.

Huggins, Janis Lindsey. *Snowmass Village, Wild at Heart: A Field Guide to Plants, Birds, & Mammals.* Town of Snowmass Village, 2008. 467 p.
> An excellent field guide to what lives in Snowmass Village today.

Johnson, Kirk, and Ray Troll. *Cruisin' the Fossil Freeway: An Epoch Tale of a Scientist and an Artist on the Ultimate 5,000-Mile Paleo Road Trip.* Golden, CO: Fulcrum Publishing, 2007. 204 p.
> The ultimate guide to fossil fun in the Rocky Mountain region.

Lange, Ian. M. *Ice Age Mammals of North America: A Guide to the Big, the Hairy, and the Bizarre.* Missoula, MT: Mountain Press, 2002. 225 p.
> A good overview of ice age animals.

Matthews, Vincent, Kate Keller Lynn, and Betty Fox. *Messages in Stone: Colorado's Colorful Geology.* Denver: Colorado Geological Survey, 2003. 157 p.
> Geologic context for the Snowmastodon discovery.

Meltzer, David J. *First Peoples in a New World: Colonizing Ice Age America.* Berkeley, CA: University of California Press, 2009. 446 p.
> Provides the background for understanding what we know about how and when people first arrived in the Americas.

INDEX

finis